HOW TO AVOID BEING
FIRED AS A PARENT

HOW TO AVOID BEING
FIRED AS
A PARENT

Building respectful relationships to secure
your family's success and happiness

JENNY BAILEY

PARTRIDGE
A Penguin Random House Company

To order additional copies of this book, contact
Toll Free 800 101 2657 (Singapore)
Toll Free 1 800 81 7340 (Malaysia)
orders.singapore@partridgepublishing.com

www.partridgepublishing.com/singapore

This book is dedicated to Rhys, without whom
I would never have travelled this journey.

TABLE OF CONTENTS

ACKNOWLEDGEMENTS

Psychologist, Dr Thomas Gordon believed strongly that using *power* was detrimental to our relationships with our children. Dr Gordon was nominated, on three accounts, for a Nobel Peace Prize for his work in developing a range of communication techniques to help us build successful relationships within these relationships. He is most famous for his development of the skills based parenting program Parent Effectiveness Training (P.E.T.).

Dr Gordon taught his first parenting program in 1962. Since then, millions of people have trained in P.E.T. skills. Since running his first program, there has been significant research into the effectiveness of the method and the benefits to both parents and children.

It is through standing on the shoulders of the work of others that modern parents can bring the best knowledge and skills and offer our own children the best psychological health and conditioning, and raise children with high Emotional Intelligence and enjoy a deep loving and trusting relationship with our own children that will endure our lifetimes. —Dr Thomas Gordon

Daniel Goleman, in his book *Emotional Intelligence,* alerted the world to the fact that Emotional Intelligence (EQ) was a better predictor of long-term success than IQ, and that emotional skills could be learned. Coleman's work heralded a stream of new insights from modern brain scientists made possible by advances in technology.

SUMMARY

We all approach parenthood along different paths. Some of us always knew we would be parents while some came here by accident. Others were swept up in the enthusiasm of their friends or family and the joy of seeing nieces and nephews come into the world.

Regardless of how we got here, we all want the best for our children, and we want to do the best parenting job. We want our children to be happy: when they are happy, we are happy. We want our children to be successful. We want them to achieve a life of which we, as their parents, can be proud.

We want to enjoy our family life. We want to take the children to the beach, play in the sand, and go on picnics and bike rides.

We want to maintain and deepen our spousal relationship by adding the joy of bringing up children together.

We want peace and quiet and for everyone to get along.

INTRODUCTION

I wrote this book because I was looking for a way of parenting that was going to enable me to build a great relationship with my child and leave me free of endless fighting about bedtime and homework and would equipment me with tools to help my child navigate the challenges of growing up.

When I started my parenting journey, I was petrified. I came from a perfectly normal middle-class background and life in Melbourne, Australia. I had two younger sisters, and my parents were totally committed to their children.

I graduated from university with an engineering degree but hated my first job in that field. I eventually became general manager at a large government business with a team of 150 members. I loved my job, was paid well and enjoyed a good life. I had a keen interest in outdoor activities and spent my weekends skiing, bike riding or paragliding. I could not think of *one* good reason to have children. Why would I want to wreck my career, send myself broke and destroy my weekends?

I fought against having children through my 20s and 30s. I saw no logical reason to have children. Clearly family life was not fun. Children cost a fortune; they destroyed your social life and disrupted opportunities to pursue your own hobbies. Children wrecked your career ….

When my husband finally announced that he wanted to have children, I was petrified. I used all of the skills I had learned in my MBA to demonstrate the *business case* for why having children did not stack up. However, deep down, in my heart, I knew I should have children. So I 'took the plunge' and gave birth to a healthy 9lb 2oz baby boy at the age of 40.

Now I really was afraid. Raising a child petrified me. Giving birth did not scare me. A few sleepless nights did not scare me. I did not want to spend my life arguing with my child and living in conflict. I wanted to know how to get him to bed without yelling. I wanted to maintain a relationship with my child. I did not want to spend life in the chaos and hostility of the families that surrounded me. Nor did I want to spend my life trying to discipline my child, only to have him yell back at me. I also had a deep-rooted fear of *screwing my child up*.

All of these fears yet I was still thinking, *How could I become the best parent I could be?*

After having my son, I looked for a parenting skills program. I found a tiny advertisement for a program called Parent Effectiveness Training (P.E.T.) in a local parenting magazine. I signed up at once and started the program when my son was only 3 months old.

The program was profound. It brought together all of the skills that I had learned during my corporate career. It put them into a comprehensive parent-child framework. I was taught how to use the skills properly. I discovered how it felt to be listened to; to be understood and to have my needs met. I discovered my needs were legitimate and that I was worthy enough to deserve to have my needs met. It felt wonderful. It was healing. I realised that how we speak to our children can not only take the conflict out of our lives but also significantly build our children's self-esteem and feelings of worthiness—how we speak to our children is powerful.

That was the gift I wanted to give to my child. It was also a gift that I would give to myself, as it would enable me to maintain my connection with my child, which would be rewarding to me. A beautiful, loving and trusting relationship is what having a child was about.

What you will find in this book

This book is for those wishing to build a strong, loving and trusting relationship with their child. It is for parents who want to raise their children without relying on threats, bribes and punishment. It is for parents who know, in their hearts, that there must be a better way of raising their children that is respectful and loving to both the child and the parent. This book will provide you with a positive and constructive way of raising your children.

This book will enable you to:

- build stronger relationships with your children, which will surpass your lifetime
- raise successful children
- avoid being fired by your children when they become teenagers
- have more of your own needs met
- enjoy more influence in your children's lives
- teach your children emotional intelligence skills

- teach your children superior communication skills
- raise emotionally secure and resilient children
- enjoy parenting.

You will discover five skill areas:

1. how to enhance your relationship with your children
2. how to help your children when they are upset or experiencing difficulties
3. how to have your own needs met without making others feel guilty
4. how to solve problems in such a way that everyone has their needs met
5. how to manage your own emotions.

This book will also address the two different aspects of our being: our emotional lives and our rational lives.

The skills and ideas described in this book are relevant to children of all ages; in fact, they are relevant to all relationships. However, most of the examples relate to children aged 2–12 years. My focus is on helping parents strengthen their relationships with their children from as young an age as possible. Teenage and older relationships can be repaired but it takes longer to rebuild lost trust that naturally comes from parenting with a system of punishment and rewards.

TRIED AND TESTED TOOLS

The skills in this book draw together a range of soundly researched bodies of work. This provides you with the confidence that this is not just *the latest fad*. Parenting books are prolific. The problem is many of them simply share the parenting experience of the person who wrote the book. It is anecdotal. It says 'this works for my child; therefore, it should work for you'. The problem with this approach is that every person is unique and every child is unique—those of you with two children already know this; you thought you knew how to look after a baby only to find that the second one is completely different.

This book draws upon the robust body of work, Parent Effectiveness Training by Dr Thomas Gordon. Dr Gordon was a counsellor, psychologist and academic. He was a contemporary of Dr Carl Rodgers who is considered the founding father of modern counselling. His first parenting class was taught over 50 years ago, and there has been plenty of research to demonstrate the effectiveness of his program.

In 2005, Daniel Goleman wrote *Emotional Intelligence: Why it can matter more than IQ*. The premise of the book was that emotional intelligence skills are a greater predictor of success than IQ, and that emotional intelligence skills can be learnt.

Following the work of Daniel Goleman, our understanding of brain science exploded through access to technology. Another significant book by Norman Doidge, *The Brain that Changes Itself* introduced the public to the concept of *neuroplasticity*. It was originally considered that the wiring of the brain was static and could not be changed. Neuroplasticity suggests that our brain can rewire itself through various means.

How to avoid being fired as a parent draws on the research of those above to present you, as parents, a comprehensive set of tools that encompasses scientific robustness and addresses both the emotional and rational sides of our and our children's being.

Many of us were parented in an Authoritarian Parenting Style and we swore that we would not parent our children in the same way. The problem is that you cannot achieve something (like raising great kids) from a position of what you are *not* going to do; it leaves you stumped for words.

Parents are looking for an alternative way of parenting that is neither authoritative nor permissive.

This book will answer your day-to-day parenting challenges. In fact, it will do more than that. It will provide you with a tried and tested way of parenting that will equip you with parenting skills that enable you to build a strong and trusting relationship with your children. It will not only prevent you from *screwing up your children,* it will arm you with the skills to be your child's *first counsellor* (the one they will come to when they are experiencing a problem) and help them navigate the challenges of growing up in a complex world.

Chapter One

THE MODERN PARENTING DILEMMA

CURRENT PARENTING CHALLENGES

You discover that by the age of four, children have their own will. Then you discover that their will is different from yours. It is usually at this stage that parents seek help: 'How do I get my kids to listen to me and do what I say?'

They start school as cute and innocent preps in their new and oversized school uniforms. They become defiant. It feels like they won't do anything they are asked. For many, family life is chaotic and not at all fun.

You have survived pre- and primary school. Now they have started high school. Your home (that is, *their* home) has turned into a war zone. The only time you see your teenager is when they want something. They come and get it (usually negotiating with their mother as she is a bigger pushover), and then they leave. If in the process you ask for something then all hell breaks loose, and there is yelling, arguments or angry sulky silences. You try to help them and provide advice on how to manage their lives. They roll their eyes, look at you like you are an imbecile and storm off. How dare you be treated like this in your own home? Where is the respect you deserve? Why will these children not take good advice? Ultimately: Where has my gorgeous little girl with the pigtails gone? Where has my little boy who used to give me cuddles gone?

You have been fired as a parent! But my message is this: major pain and conflict is not necessary when children become teenagers.

Over the years, I have spoken to thousands of parents of pre- and primary school children. During these interactions, I discovered there are clear and common challenges, of which there are millions of variations on the theme:

- How do I deal with my children's meltdowns, tantrums and upsets?
- My children don't listen to me.
- My children are fighting all the time.
- How do I manage myself and stop yelling at my children?

Parents these days are acutely aware that the way they parent really matters for their children's long-term emotional and psychological health. A parent's greatest fear is that they are going to *screw up* their children. They know this because they are aware that how they were treated as children has impacted their adult life, or they have seen evidence of this in others.

THE IMPORTANCE OF NEEDS FOR OUR FAMILY'S SURVIVAL

Both parents and children have needs, and they deserve to have their needs met. We are all driven, psychologically and biologically, to have our needs met for survival.

The Parent Effectiveness Model below shows the four types of families (based on their parenting style) and how they are going about having their needs met.

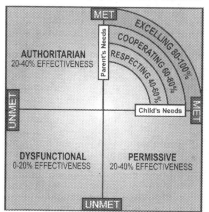

PARENTING EFFECTIVENESS MODEL

In the bottom left quadrant neither the parents nor the children are having their needs met. This family is Dysfunctional. The symptoms are frustrated parents and frustrated children. Parents are unable to help their children and are inattentive to their needs. They don't listen to their children, who tend to be highly emotional, and either upset or angry. They don't listen to their parents.

In the bottom right quadrant, we have Permissive families. Here the children are having their needs met but the parents are not. The parents are being *walked all over*. The children are not considerate of the parents, and could be considered spoilt. The problem with these families is that over time the parents become resentful when their needs are not being met. They begin to dislike their children. The problem for the children is they don't learn to be considerate of other people's needs. They also start to feel resentment towards their parents.

In the top right quadrant, we have Authoritarian families. In these families, the parents have their needs met but the children do not. These are families where children should be *seen and not heard* and where you might hear, 'You are living in my house and my rules apply'. Parents generally get what they want but the children don't. The children might be *compliant* and do what they are told to *please* their parents. Other children will become *defiant*. These children fight back against their parents. They become aggressive and badly behaved. They won't do what they are told despite threats and punishment.

Children in these families often grow up feeling their needs are not important or don't matter. They feel they are not listened to. Often they will grow up feeling alone with their problems.

We are programmed to behave a certain way in order to have our needs met. If we can't ask for help, we will try to have our needs met in other, less direct ways—you could call these ways *manipulative*. This family model will seem familiar to many of us.

Finally, we have the top right quadrant. Here parents and children are respectful of each other's needs, and recognise that having their individual needs met does not mean someone else has to miss having their needs met. It is not a 'zero-sum' game. There are ways of relating to each other where parents can have their needs met and so can their children. Some take these concepts further and cooperate to help everyone to have their needs met.

In truly successful families, all members are actively engaged in having their own needs met and helping other family members have their needs met. Can you imagine growing up in a family where everyone else was actively committed to helping you have your needs met and be successful? Can you imagine being a parent in a family where your children were actively engaged in helping you be successful at what you want in life? No longer do mothers have to sacrifice 20 years of their lives to raise children. No longer do children grow up feeling that they are not very important.

Parents don't know any better

In my parenting seminars, I begin by asking parents: 'In your many years of formal and informal education have you ever undertaken a parenting program?' The majority answer no. I then ask them how they have developed their parenting style if they have not embarked on a program. Almost unanimously, they say they must have learned their parenting style from their parents.

For most of us this rings true. How often do you hear yourself sounding exactly like your parents? Sobering, isn't it? Surely, we are more than just our parents. In addition, most of us swore that, as parents, we would never say these things to our children.

The truth is the majority of us parent as our parents parented us. It is what we know. Our parents parented as their parents did and so on, back through the generations. In reality, we are parenting using ancient methods. There might be nothing wrong with this except that over the past 60 years there has been significant research into the nature of human relationships and parenting: what works and what does not. In most areas of our society, we do not relate to others by controlling them with punishment and rewards. Physical punishment is only used against children. In the workplace, we focus on engaging our employees – not punishing them.

Many parents would adopt a No-Lose approach to parenting if they understood the impact of their Authoritarian methods and were taught the alternative.

Losing power

Many parents are fearful of losing their power and influence over their children if they stop using it.

I also suspect that those who felt powerless as children feel it is important to retain power as a parent – otherwise they feel that they lose power at both ends. What few realise is that their power is transitory; it is short lived. By giving up their power, they gain influence – much more valuable in the long term.

My friends do it this way

The culture in which we live is a very powerful determinate of our behaviour. The way we raise our children can often be very public. There are many people watching how you are dealing with your badly behaving child. We are particularly vulnerable to the judgements of others when we lack confidence in our parenting abilities, and many parents lack this confidence.

The pressure to punish your children can be hard to resist. Teachers often speak to the parents when a child has behaved badly. They will have generally already punished the child themselves but seem to expect you as the parents to at least give them another lecture.

Parental influence: I raised four kids and they are fine

Our own parents can also be quite judgemental towards our parenting style. After all, we do have to admit that they have been parents. If we claim they did a bad job then we are criticising ourselves.

All parents want to be good parents. It was the same for our parents. Many wonder: could I have done a better job? What could I have done differently? They look at their children's problems and character defects and ask, *is that my fault*? What could/should I have done differently? Having their children choose to parent differently than they did makes them feel defensive. Having their children choose to parent the same way they did gives them some confidence that what they did was correct.

I remember sitting with a 70-year-old woman whose five adult children were all lacking in confidence. 'What should I have done differently?' she lamented with tears in her eyes. 'It must be my fault.'

My parents smacked me, and I'm OK

Parents adopt the parenting style of their parents by arguing that, 'My parents brought me up this way, and I'm OK!' Let's face it: who wants to admit that they are *not* OK?

Many parents still smack their children. A 2010 American study showed that one in five parents still smack their children to manage misbehaviour. Many parents say, 'My parents smacked me and I'm OK'.

Effort to learn something new

Even once parents realise there is a better way to raise their children than using an Authoritarian Parenting Style, there is often reluctance to change. Inertia is a big factor in getting people to change their parenting style. It takes time and effort. Parents are very time poor. Adults do not want to learn something new until there is a real need. Unfortunately, for many parents, they do not realise the importance of changing their parenting style until it is too late – and the kids have already fired you as a parent.

Some parents are lucky. They get a defiant or rebellious child. Their household is in chaos already. They have to do something and realise they have to change their parenting style. They come along to classes, put in the effort to learn the parenting skills and change. They are rewarded with an infinitely more peaceful family and insurance against being fired by their children when they become parents.

We don't want to parent the way our parents did

When we were children, our parents told us what to do and we did it. They enforced threats and punishments to manage our actions. Many of us were punished physically if we transgressed the rules set in the house. Often we were fearful of our parents. We did not want to be in trouble so we tended to not confide in them. This meant we often did not have anyone to turn to if we needed help. Growing up, for some, was a lonely place. If something was going wrong at school or with their friends, their parents were not there to help them.

There are few people who enter parenthood *without* a clear idea of how they *want* to parent but *with* a clear idea of how they do *not* want to parent. Their parenting style therefore, tends to be defined by doing the opposite of what their parents did.

Today, rather than punishing our children we encourage them with rewards. We introduce reward charts then feel resentful at having to use bribery to get them to do the most basic things. We do not want to be harsh, like our parents, so often we end up being *walked all over*. Then we get mad and resort to our parent's style of Authoritarian parenting: we punish our kids and then feel guilty. Then the cycle starts again.

THIS WORLD IS NOT THE WORLD OF OUR CHILDHOOD

Another confusing parenting dilemma is that our own experiences of growing up are not transferable to the modern world. I certainly remember how useless I found my parent's advice about what *they* did when *they* were growing up. The gap between *our* childhood and *our children's* childhood is even bigger. The advent of hand-held devices and games has totally changed the landscape of being a child. When we were kids, we talked about what we watched on TV last night. Now our children are totally engaged in the language and the world of Minecraft, Clash of Clans and Total Girl.com.

I received an email from my son, with a photo of what had happened in class. The photo was taken with his iPad. As parents, we are petrified about the effect screen time is having on our children. Yet, I remember my mother's conversations with other mothers about watching too much TV and how they were fearful we would grow up with square eyes.

Jobs that never existed years ago are now part of our present, whereas, many jobs that exist now are quickly disappearing. The disruption to our society will continue and we know most of our children will have multiple careers. Our educators don't seem to know whether to stick to *chalk and talk* or sit our children in front of online learning to enable them to progress. What do they need to learn anyway? Do they really need to handwrite?

Too much advice?

Parents today are bombarded with parenting books and advice from all angles—many of which are contradictory. Our parents judge the way we parent our children, in the same way they judged *us* when we were children. Teachers assume when our children misbehave at school it must be our fault as parents. Our friends watch us interact with our children. Even David Cameron blamed parents for the 2011 riots in London—everyone has an opinion.

Is it any wonder we are confused and lack confidence?

The four styles of parenting

There are four types of parenting styles and according to clinical and developmental psychologist Diana Baumrind, you are one over the other depending upon whether you are demanding or undemanding of your child and whether you are responsive or unresponsive to your child's needs and wishes.

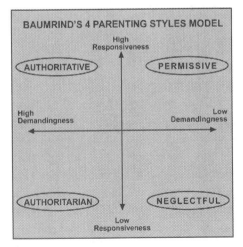

Authoritarian Parenting Style

The most common style of parenting in western society is Authoritarian. Dr Louise Porter (a prominent Australian psychologist) uses the phrase *controlling discipline* (Porter D. L., 2014) to describe this style of parenting which is characterised by the following:

- Children's behaviour should be managed and controlled by the parent.
- Children will not do the right thing unless you tell them what to do.
- Children should be obedient.
- Children should respect you because you are their parent.
- You can control children's behaviour by punishing (or threatening to punish) or through rewards.
- Children can be trained to do the right thing, for example, if you tell them repeatedly to say please and withhold what the child wants until they say please, then that is how they will eventually learn to say please and learn manners.
- It is a parent's job to set boundaries (rules) and to enforce by punishment.
- Parents know what is best and make all decisions for the child – the parent is the boss.

There are significant downsides to this method of parenting, for both the parent and child, which will be discussed in the following chapter in this book.

Authoritative or No-Lose Parenting Style

There is a range of different names used to describe this type of parenting. I have chosen the term No-Lose

Parenting as described by Dr Thomas Gordon. Other names for this parenting style includes Democratic or Authoritative (Baumrind) or the Guidance Approach (Porter). A No-Lose Parenting Style is characterised by:

- A recognition that rewards and punishment don't work to manage children's behaviour.
- Children behave to get their needs met and are not inherently naughty or bad.
- Mistakes by children are inevitable because they have so much to learn, and mistakes are an integral part of learning.
- Children, who are respected and listened to, will be respectful and considerate of their parents.
- Children inherently want to please their parents.
- Children need control over their own lives and do not want to be controlled.
- Boundaries (or rules) are negotiated based on both the parent and child's needs.
- Open and authentic communication is critical.

The aim of parenting is to guide children towards their own independence rather than to control them. This book teaches this style of parenting.

Permissive Parenting Style

A Permissive Parenting Style is characterised by:

- low expectations of the child
- few or no boundaries
- child can do what they want.

Permissive parenting is when children get what they want at the expense of the parents. Although permissive parenting may appear to be the alternative to the Authoritarian parenting with which we grew up, we seem to know intuitively that it is not the answer either. Those of us who have tried find it does not work. We become resentful and angry towards our children if we feel that we are being walked all over.

Neglectful Parenting Style

Neglectful Parenting Style is characterised by having low expectations of the child and not meeting the child's needs.

It is unlikely that neglectful parents will be taking the time to read a parenting book such as this one, so we will not discuss this style any further.

However, the majority of parents use an Authoritarian style of parenting which will inevitably cause your children to fire you as a parent when they become teenagers – let's explore why.

Chapter Two

THE IMPACT OF USING POWER TO PARENT

WHAT IS A SYSTEM OF PUNISHMENT AND REWARDS?

The Authoritarian system of punishment and rewards can be considered the *carrot and the stick*.

Children are punished when they do something wrong in the anticipation they will not do it again. They are threatened with punishment if they undertake an *undesirable* behaviour, and are rewarded when they do something correct, to encourage that same behaviour to continue. The theoretical root of this method is behaviourism, which states that a person's behaviour is a response to external stimulus.

PUNISHMENT AND REWARDS REQUIRE THE USE OF PARENTAL POWER

As parents, we have power over young children, which mean we have the power to punish them. We have the power to deny them material needs and wants, for example, take away their favourite toy, send them to bed without dinner, or withhold their pocket money. We can also deny them their emotional needs such as putting them in timeout, sending them to their room, not allowing them to visit their friends and saying hurtful things. In more extreme cases, we kick them out of home or become violent towards our children through smacking.

We also have significant power to reward our children as we control most of the economic resources of the family. We can do this with chocolate, toys and trips to their favourite places.

PUNISHMENT DOES NOT WORK AS A PREVENTATIVE STRATEGY

Punishing children to ensure good behaviour does not work. How can that be? Firstly, if punishment worked then why is it always the same children who go to the principal's office, get punished for their misbehaviour and are back again the following week?

Punishment does not elicit good behaviour. You have already had to tolerate the poor behaviour. Punishment occurs after the fact. It does not cause good behaviour.

OK, you say, it will stop them behaving badly next time. Will it? Or will the child just make sure you don't see them next time? After all, you can only punish poor behaviours when you are present. How are you going to manage your child's behaviour with punishment, when you are not there to witness it?

OK, you say, I will just threaten to punish, that will stop them. The problem with this argument is you will now be required to anticipate all of the poor behaviours that could be exhibited and then threaten punishment for any or all of them. You will have to be there to monitor the behaviour so you can punish if the behaviour is exhibited. Doesn't sound very practical, does it?

Punishment does not work, as the child still does not know why their behaviour was unacceptable. The reason for their (mis)behaviour most likely still exists. At the end of the punishment, the child will probably make a resolution to ensure they are not caught next time. They are unlikely to make a resolution to change their behaviour.

THE PROBLEM WITH PUNISHMENT

Using punishment or threats of punishment may work for your child in the short term but there are downsides of this for parents.

Enforcing punishment is also hard work for parents as it costs valuable time and effort to implement the punishment. For example, if the parent bans their child from TV for the week, they have to be vigilant about monitoring their child to ensure they do not watch TV. It also might not suit you to have to enforce the ban. Maybe you would prefer the TV to be on so you can get some peace and quiet, but you can't because you feel you have to follow up your punishment. Implementing punishment is like putting a heavy load on your back—on top of the already heavy load of raising your children.

When we punish our children, we feel distant from them. They feel bad and so do we. This makes us more emotionally distant from them and we are more likely to think of them negatively. There is less warmth in our interactions with our children. We might find ourselves yelling at them or forcing them to do something they don't want to do, or taking away from them something that is very important to them like a favourite toy or the opportunity to watch their favourite TV show. It's like driving a wedge between you and your children.

Punishing our children can make us feel guilty. However, it is fair to say that some people don't feel much guilt when they punish their children and others feel much more—it is very personality dependent.

When we punish our children, we know in our deepest heart that we have hurt them and in the process, we hurt ourselves. It is like drinking poison and expecting our children to behave better.

There are many stories of parents who are so hurt because their children will not let them see their grandchildren. There are many stories of grown-up children that treat their parents badly. I had a woman in one of my classes who had grown up to be abusive towards her mother. She continued to take advantage of her mother, including dumping her 2-year-old child on her to raise. Why did the mother put up with this? It was due to the state of her heart and the fact she wanted to look after her daughter and grandchild. I am sure you can imagine how much pain it must cause a mother to be treated so badly by her daughter.

THE PROBLEM WITH THREATS

Threatening our children is toxic to our relationship with them.

When we threaten our children, they may or may not do as we wish and if they don't then we may or may not chose to follow up our threat with punishment.

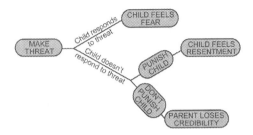

If we threaten our child and they respond to our threat by doing what is required, we may initially feel triumphant. We have achieved what we need to achieve. Threatening our children works most of the time for some children, often for others and never for some. Threatening our children comes at a high price.

If your children do what you want, is it because they are afraid of your threats? If this is the case, they become fearful of you. It is very difficult to build a close relationship with someone whom you fear. Nor do we want to raise children who remain constantly fearful. They then become people who spend their mental capacity working out how to keep themselves safe instead of working out how they can help others or learn and build their own capabilities. Every threat that generates fear is like dosing our children with a tablespoon of poison that slowly kills their feelings of wellbeing.

If your children do not do what you want them to do (when you threaten them), you have two choices:

1. follow through on the threat
2. do not follow through on the threat.

Both options have significant downsides.

Should we decide not to follow through on our threat, the result is you no longer become believable. You have lost your credibility in the eyes of your child. Your children will see you as someone who does not keep their word. Given that children model their parents' relationship style, they will learn to make promises they cannot keep. It is like burning out the phone lines so no meaningful words come through the system. You may as well put a big sign on your forehead that says, 'Don't believe a word I say'. If you are not believable (on your threats), you are probably not believable on everything else you say. Your children will tune out and not listen to you.

It is no wonder the old saying hasn't evolved, 'Don't make threats that you are not prepared to carry out'. I would suggest you stop making threats. If they work, it is at the cost of your children fearing you. If they don't and you don't follow through you become someone whom they don't believe. If you do choose to carry out threats, you will experience all of the downsides of punishment. Making any sort of threat to your children is toxic to your relationship with them.

THE PROBLEM WITH REWARDS

A system of rewards *can* work to get desired behaviours from our children but there are multiple problems for parents when they use such a system to raise their children. In the past decade, many parents have opted for rewards instead of punishment, as we have felt increasingly more uncomfortable with punishing our children. However, there are many downsides to using rewards: it is costly and hard work to implement; it increases our child's dependency on us, and can ultimately lead us to become resentful.

A system of rewards is hard work to implement. It requires us to:

- decide the behaviour that we want
- determine what currency will work for the child

- require us to design the rewards system
- implement the system.

Firstly, the parent has to decide what behaviour they want to encourage. It might be learning to spell better, making their beds or eating their vegetables.

Then the parent has to work out what motivates the child. Do they want chocolate frogs, gold stars, money or more stories at bedtime? It can become quite difficult to work out the *currency* that works for your child, and to make things more difficult, it changes over time. When children reach four years of age they may very well be motivated by gold stars on reward charts but this will not motivate a 7- or 12-year-old.

It is then necessary to determine how to design the reward system. How are you going to monitor and track the behaviours that you want to see? Do you need charts? Who will update them? Who decides whether the task has been delivered to a suitable quality?

Finally, you need to implement the system, monitor the behaviour, add the stars, and purchase the reward when enough points have been earned.

I was persuaded by an educator to implement a reward system to encourage my 8-year-old to practise his handwriting. Against my better judgement, I agreed to it. It required 10 minutes per day for 6 weeks. My child negotiated an Xbox as a reward (I can't believe that I agreed to that!) The whole process was exceedingly painful. You would like to think that with such a reward my child would get up each morning to practise. But no. He still had to be persuaded and cajoled. There was very little work done in the 10 minutes due to procrastination and other avoidance techniques. I even found myself reading to him while he practised. After all that, his handwriting is still appalling and I promised I would never agree to such an arrangement again.

The system of rewards is also costly. It generally requires the payment of material goods such as toys, treats or privileges they would otherwise not get. We have to control things they want access to so we can leverage it as a reward, or provide extra resources. However, is it necessary to *pay* our children to do things they should be doing anyway with items they would otherwise not get? Rewards get more and more costly as the child grows older. Pre-school children might be happy with gold stars and chocolate frogs but 10-year-olds want footy cards, computer games or new clothes. Most of us cannot afford what teenagers want. Parenting with rewards will grow a hole in your wallet.

I will never forget working at a fundraiser at my child's primary school. The grade 6 children were working as servers. I said to one boy's mother that I thought he had done a great job. He immediately turned to his mother and said, 'What do I get for that?'

Over time, the effort and cost of implementing a system of rewards can cause parents to become resentful towards their children. 'Why should I have to pay them to do things that they should do anyway?' The trouble with resentment is it undermines our relationship with our children. It slowly drives a wedge between them and us. If we are annoyed with them, we are more likely to have sharp words with them. Over time, our relationship can become distant and we miss the depth of love that could exist.

The final downside of a system of rewards is it trains children to be dependent upon external rewards for their motivation. Children do things because they are going to *get something* (externally) rather than looking internally for their motivation to act. In psychology, there is a concept called intrinsic versus extrinsic motivation. **Extrinsically motivated** people look outside themselves for their rewards.

If you have ever managed staff you will notice extrinsically motivated people because they will only do things that are on their performance plan, and if they think they will be rewarded for it. They don't *step in* to do things because they cannot see the worth in the action. **Intrinsically motivated** people do things because they think they are inherently worthwhile.

Teaching a child to be extrinsically motivated is like taking the rudder and motor out of a boat and letting it be pushed around by the external forces of wind and waves. The impact of this, on the parents, is they find they need to step in more and more to push the child in the right direction – until finally they realise they can't do this anymore because it is exhausting and *it does not work*.

Parental power runs out when children become teenagers

It is impossible to punish our children once they become teenagers. We cannot physically put them in time out. We cannot take away their favourite toy. We cannot physically stop them seeing their friends. We cannot smack a 5 foot 7, 15-year-old boy.

Providing rewards also becomes impossible. What does your child want that you don't have, that could be used as a reward? Maybe an iPad, if you can afford one. Once they have the iPad they are not going to do what you want them to do at the promise of another iPad.

I often show parents a chocolate frog at my seminars. I tell them that chocolate frogs are magic, that you can get a 4-year-old to do amazing things for a chocolate frog. But what self-respecting 15-year-old is going to do what you want them to do at the promise of a chocolate frog?

In 2011, Amy Chua released a book called *Battle Hymn of the Tiger Mother*. The following was written on the front cover, 'This is a story about a mother, two daughters, and two dogs. This was *supposed* to be a story of how Chinese parents are better at raising kids than Western ones. But instead, it's about a bitter clash of cultures, a fleeting taste of glory, and how I was humbled by a thirteen-year-old'.

It is a powerful book—beautifully written and breathtakingly honest. It describes the fantastic academic and musical achievements of her children followed by how her 13-year-old daughter effectively fired her as a parent at the intense emotional cost to both mother and daughter. I was particularly struck by the fact it was exactly when the child became a teenager that she started to exert her own power, and her mother had no more power to exert in order to control her daughter.

Why controlling our children causes a loss of control

We just want well-behaved children. Authoritarian parents believe that to see considerate behaviour we need to control our children's behaviour (with punishment and rewards).

When we try to control our children, we teach them they should simply *do what we say*. We believe that if our children do what we say, they will be safe and successful. There are several problems with this belief.

If we control our children to do exactly as we say, we are ultimately sending them *to sea*. They will not know what to do without a parent instructing them, will start asking *any* adult for instruction and will lack initiative. All this can be very stressful for them as they lack the confidence to be able to make decisions. Those of you who have ever managed staff will have encountered employees who lack initiative and are constantly coming to you for instruction. Then they come looking for praise. These people lack initiative and are extrinsically motivated (seek external rewards) rather than intrinsically motivated (doing things because you want to and see value in them). These employees were most likely parented by controlling parents.

If we expect our children to do what we say without argument, we are also teaching them to do what other adults say. We may be happy for our children to do what their teacher or even other parent's say, but children who have been trained to do what adults say, without argument, will also tend to succumb to the controlling power of peers. Do you really want your children to bypass their own good sense and do what everyone else does or says? Will they be safe? Will they be capable of resisting peer pressure?

Training your children to be obedient reduces their safety and leaves them open to abuse and manipulation by others.

We want considerate, not compliant children

If our children are compliant, we have to work out what they should be doing and instruct them continuously. This requires enormous effort and is ultimately an impossible task. It's a bit like making your own coffee rather than ordering it from the barista.

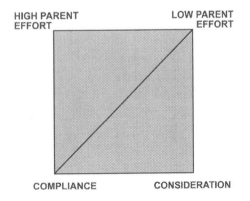

What we really want are considerate children, those who don't have to be told what to do and regard the needs of others. This becomes especially important as the age to move out of home reaches 30+! You want to live with considerate housemates, not ones whom you have to ask constantly to empty the dishwasher and pick up their clothes from the lounge room floor.

When my child was 8 we had his grandparents over to stay. My son wanted to watch the TV. He came to me and said, 'Mum do you know where the head phones are because I want to watch my favourite show and I know that Grandma and Grandpa won't like the noise.'

THE IMPORTANCE OF RELATIONSHIPS

Good relationships increase our enjoyment of life; however, they are much more important than that. Numerous studies have shown that people with strong relationships and social connections experience significantly improved mental and physical health. Good relationships are like a strong tonic.

Good relationships with our children are essential for us as parents. After all, why did we have children? Apart from a basic biological drive, I believe we had children because we were looking to have a good relationship with them—to give them love and to feel the love in return. A breakdown in the relationship with our child can cause deep heartache. Many of us dream of the joy of having our families together for special celebrations.

However, the reality for many parents is their children just don't want to hang out with them. Their children tolerate them rather than want to be with them as they feel obligated to spend time with their parents, but would prefer not to. Is that how you want your relationship with your children to be? Do you want to hear their angry and hurtful words or see them storming off after an argument with you? Do you want access to your grandchildren?

I often notice the cries of grandparents, *I can't see my grandchildren. My daughter or son won't let me.* The pain is deep for these grandparents, compounded by the difficulties of the daughter- or son-in-law.

Trust and relationships

Trust is essential to build a good relationship with our children. Trust is defined as 'firm belief in the truth, reliability, or ability of someone or something' (Oxford Dictionary, 2006). Trust is like cement to the relationship.

When our children are born, they have no choice but to trust us. If they cannot trust us enough to meet their basic needs, they will die. Critical elements of trust are:

- predictability
- reliability
- honesty.

Power undermines trust

Using power undermines the trust our children have placed in us. They are biologically wired to trust us and their survival is dependent upon it. Every time we use power, threats, punishment or rewards we damage this trust.

When we put our child in timeout, they learn they cannot trust us to be there when they need us. When we take away their favourite toy, they learn they cannot trust us not to hurt them. When we physically hurt them, they learn they cannot trust us to keep them safe.

Using power with our children is like letting white ants eat away at the foundations of your relationship.

INFLUENCE

As parents, we want to be able to influence our children to make the right choices, keep them safe and adopt the values we think are important. We cannot use power to achieve influence. We may be able to use power to coerce or make our children do what we want but we cannot make them change the way they think. What we actually want is to be able to influence their thinking and help them decide on the right choices rather than have us decide what is best for them and make them do it.

The only way to achieve influence is to have a good relationship with our children. Think about someone who has influenced you. Did you have a good relationship with them?

Trust and a good relationship are required for influence. Parents who use power to raise their children find they undermine the trust their children have in them and the influence they have over them.

Using power to raise our children is like putting acid on our trust—it eats away at our influence.

I once visited home, during a break from university, when my mum handed me an invitation to my school reunion. *She* wanted me to go and for the life of me I still don't know why. The only power she had left, with a university-aged child was guilt. She said, 'Won't you do it for me?' The answer was, 'No way'. Upon reflection, my mother never communicated her reasons for wanting me to go; however, I can only assume she had good intentions. I never communicated to her my reasons for not wanting to go. I suspect if we had communicated properly, I still would not have gone, but we would have understood one another better. Instead, she felt thwarted and I felt guilty.

Chapter Three

PARENTING FOR YOUR CHILD'S EMOTIONAL HEALTH

Psychological and emotional health

Relationships with others are strongly correlated with physical and mental health and wellbeing.

Our ability to develop strong relationships with others is also a key predictor to how successful we will be. We are biologically programed to build relationships with others, without which our survival is at risk. We learn to build relationships with others based on our first experiences of building relationships with our parents.

'Dozens of studies have shown that people who have satisfying relationships with family, friends, and their community are happier, have fewer health problems, and live longer.' (Havard Health Publications, 2001)

The biggest predictor of your child's long-term wellbeing, emotional and psychological health is the quality of their critical relationship with their parents. Building strong relationships with your children is like giving them a vaccination against depression, and their emotional system an injection of steroids.

'The family and the relationships within have a huge influence on a child's well-being and emotional development and their ability to cope with situations, challenges, relationships and living.' (Helpline, 2015)

'Of the many different relationships people form over the course of the life span, the relationship between parent and child is among the most important.' (Health)

EMOTIONAL INTELLIGENCE

Goleman's book on *Emotional Intelligence* challenged the accepted belief that IQ is the key to success. Goleman coined the term EQ to cover Emotional Intelligence. He defined five key elements:

- knowing own emotions
- manage own emotions
- motivate self
- recognise others' emotions
- handle relationships.

Goleman motioned that these skills were predictors of a successful life and could be learned. They were not innate elements, such as what IQ was believed to be at the time. These skills are not taught in schools. They are learned at home from parents.

Teaching emotional intelligence skills to your child builds a strong foundation for their future success; helps secure their future happiness; and equips them with skills in emotional intelligence. However, for you to teach these skills, you must know them, practise them and model them for your children.

The skills, described in this book, will teach *your* children to understand their own emotions and will teach *you* how to communicate your emotions to your child so that they learn to recognise others' emotions. These skills will improve your own ability to build relationships and model this for your children.

PUNISHMENT AND RESENTMENT

The main impact of punishment on children is anger and resentment, which may be repressed or expressed. Each punishment chips away at the child's self-esteem. Each punishment is a tiny drop of acid on their flesh, which will settle into a large, red, angry wound. Every time a child is subjected to the power of the parent, they feel helpless and frustrated. Each punishment decreases trust, increases the emotional distance between parent and child, and drives a wedge between them. Sometimes the anger turns inwards and is stored for later, and sometimes it is expressed outwards in angry deeds and acts. Anger is compressed resentment and frustration.

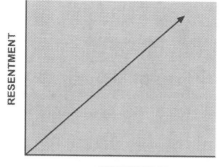

WHAT CAUSES UNDESIRABLE BEHAVIOUR

Punishment and rewards cause your children to behave badly.

Using punishment and rewards will cause your child to develop undesirable habits and behaviours. When people (not just children) are subject to threats such as punishment, they tend to respond in three possible ways:

1. fight
2. flight
3. submit.

Fight

Many people attend my seminars and programs because they have defiant children. I hear:

1. My first child is a delight but my second is defiant.
2. S/he will not do as they are told.
3. That is why I am here: can you tell me how to get my child to do as s/he is told?

These defiant children are choosing to fight the controlling discipline. Their need for autonomy is greater than their need for a good relationship with you so they choose to fight. Fighting controlling discipline can take many forms and children fighting a system of punishment and rewards can exhibit the following behaviours:

- anger
- hostility
- aggression
- retaliation
- resistance
- defiance
- rebellion
- negativity
- resentment
- striking back
- lying
- being bossy
- bullying
- being overly competitive
- ganging up on the parents.

Flight

Another way of coping with punishment and rewards is *flight* – running away. It is not obvious to us that these children are having difficulty because they don't tell us; therefore, all looks well on the outside.

Children who choose this coping strategy exhibit the following behaviours:

- lying
- hiding feelings
- blaming others

- tattling
- cheating
- withdrawing
- escaping
- fantasising
- regression
- fear of trying something new
- extrinsically rather than intrinsically motivated
- loss of connection with self.

Submit

These children simply submit to a system of punishment and rewards. Their behaviours include:
- submission
- obedience (to everyone, not just you)
- complying (to everyone's requests, not just yours)
- withdrawing
- loss of initiative
- conformity
- lack of creativity
- fear of trying something new
- extrinsically rather than intrinsically motivated
- dependent
- loss of authenticity.

We don't want these behaviours. We want **confident** and **considerate** children.

Defiance and compliance

Using power to control children will lead to one of two predictable responses—that of compliance or defiance. Children have many needs, one of which is to please their parents, to be approved of or to be OK. Another is the need for some independence or control over their life. How a child responds to parental power will depend upon which of these needs is more important for your child.

If your child has a higher need for independence, they will chose defiance. If the child has a greater need for approval, they will chose compliance. Compliance and defiance are different sides of the same coin.

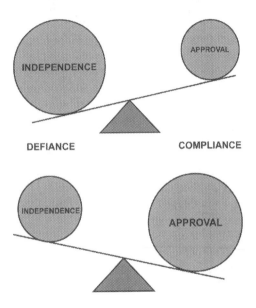

Defiant children

All children have needs. In addition to food, shelter and love, our children need a degree of autonomy and privacy. They do not enjoy being told what to do all of the time. For some children, their need for independence and control is greater than their need to be accepted by you. This need, combined with parents using power to manage their children's behaviour, leads to what is often described as *defiant* behaviour. For these children, it's like choosing a hard life of freedom rather than the physical comforts of a dry bed and 3 meals a day in jail.

These are the children, from whom you can take away a favourite toy and they say, 'I don't care'. These children can scream at you and leave the house at the age of 5. They can throw and break things. Typical behaviours of a defiant child are arguing back, ignoring instructions and anger.

Defiant children are open to diagnosis of Oppositional Defiance Disorder (ODD). 'Oppositional Defiant Disorder is a childhood disorder that is characterised by negative, defiant, disobedient and often hostile behaviour toward adults and authority figures primarily.' (Central, 2013)

Children for whom their independence and autonomy is paramount, see fighting against power and control to be as normal as the human need to eat.

Complaint children

Other children faced with the same parenting style are *compliant*. Their need to be liked and accepted by you is greater than their need for autonomy or control over their lives. They respond to parental power with *compliance*. They do what they are told. They don't rock the boat. It is interesting there is no mental disorder ascribed to compliant children—maybe there should be. Imagine raising a child to ignore their own internal compass and judgement as to correct behaviour and rather look for a source of authority (another person or parent) in order to know what to do from one minute to the next. It would be like removing a boat's motor and letting the wind and waves direct it.

Consequences

There are a range of negative consequences to children who are parented in the Authoritarian style. These include:

- risk of control by others
- eating disorders
- loss of self.

The symptoms of *Compliance Disorder* may not manifest themselves fully, for years.

Compliant children and sexual abuse

Sexual abuse of children is a widely discussed topic. It is really beyond comprehension as to how abuse of children is so widespread and has been for such a long time. How could this have happened?

Frieda Briggs, a professor in early childhood, interviewed paedophiles and asked them how they managed to get away with the abuse that they perpetrated. The most common answer was that they would not have been able to get away with it if parents had not trained their children to do what adults say. 'It's dangerous because if we teach children to do as they're told they're vulnerable to abuse particularly sexual abuse'. (Porter L., 2004)

Compliant children and loss of self

Compliant children respond to parenting power by abdicating belief in themselves, and belief in what they think is right. In the beginning, this is toward a parent. Later it might be toward a boss or a partner. This results in a profound loss of self.

As children, they do not *appear* to suffer any problems. Because they are *compliant,* they do everything that is required of them from listening to parents and teachers and choosing a sensible university course to study. These children will leave university and get a good job. Parents can pat themselves on the back in the belief they have done a good job. They can hold their heads up high when talking to the other parents.

As adults, they appear to do well (in early adulthood). Problems occur later in life when they may experience a range of symptoms:

- feel disconnected from themselves
- find themselves in a career that they are not really interested in
- career has stalled
- midlife crisis
- a feeling that they have pleased everyone else but not themselves
- overall feelings of discontentment and unhappiness
- cynicism about work and life.

These issues take considerable effort to address and can mean years of unhappiness and discontentment for the compliant adult, all with a negative impact on those around them.

Compliant children and eating disorders

There is evidence to suggest that an Authoritative Parenting Style is a contributing factor to the development of eating disorders.

'Eating disorder scores were significantly and positively correlated with patient's perception of the father as authoritarian and inversely correlated with her perception of him as authoritative.' (Enten & Golan)

IMPORTANCE OF ACCEPTANCE

Acceptance of your children is essential for their long-term health and wellbeing. We cannot support our children if we are striving for them to be different. They will feel judged and will likely develop an internal mindset that says they are not OK as they are. This is a dreadful legacy to leave with a child.

'It is one of those simple but true paradoxes in life: When a person feels truly accepted by another, as he is, then he is free to think about how he wants to change, how he wants to grow, how he can become different, how he might become more of what he is capable of being.' Dr Thomas Gordon.

THE IMPORTANCE OF TRUST IN A RELATIONSHIP

As humans, we are only influenced by those with whom we have a good relationship. Think about it. Can you think of someone you don't like or respect? Would you willingly do as they say?

No, you wouldn't. You don't like your boss yet you have to do what they say because they have *power* over you. They are ultimately able to fire you from a job that supports your mortgage and your ability to put food on the table.

So try again. Can you think of anyone, whom you dislike or trust, where you would willingly do as they say? I expect the answer is still no. So try this...Think of someone by whom you are influenced, someone you emulate or model yourself against. Do you trust them? Do you respect them? Do you have a good relationship with them?

You *are influenced* by someone whom you trust and have a relationship. You *are not influenced* by someone with whom you don't trust, respect or have a relationship.

You will only influence your children if they trust, respect and have a warm relationship with you. Every time you punish your child, you damage your relationship with them. More punishment equals less influence.

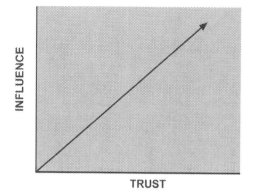

Influence is 'the capacity to have an effect on the character, development, or behaviour of someone or something, or the effect itself'. (Dictionary, 2006) We want to influence our children. We want to mould their character, and behaviour.

Every time we use a system of punishment and rewards to raise our children and control their behaviour, we undermine our relationship with them; damage hard-earned trust and ultimately, destroy any influence we may have in their lives.

Chapter Four

THE PHILOSOPHY AND MINDSET OF THE RESPECTFUL PARENT

This chapter describes the philosophy and mindset required to be a respectful parent and build a great relationship with your child.

STOP USING POWER

One of the most important philosophies of the respectful parent is the understanding that every time you use power to get what you want, you undermine your relationship with your child and it will likely cause a psychological wound. So stop using power. Stop punishing your children. Now.

And yes, there is an alternative to using power to raise your children; an alternative that will not involve raising spoilt, selfish children or leave you feeling like a slave to your children. Sure you might have to rugby tackle your three-year-old, if they are about to walk under a moving truck, but it's only on these rare, life-threatening occasions that you need to use parental power.

Using threats, punishment and rewards to get basic things done—clean teeth, put shoes on, get homework done—has a corrosive effect on your relationship with your child. By using this approach continually, they will see you as someone not to be trusted or someone to be feared. They won't confide in you for fear of being punished. They will behave in undesirable ways to keep themselves safe and to have their needs met. They will feel unsupported and may feel unloved. They will feel alone in the world. They may believe they are not good enough.

UNDERSTANDING CHILDREN'S BEHAVIOUR

Meeting needs

A respectful parent understands that children don't misbehave, they simply behave in a certain way to have their needs met. Like parents, children experience the same basic needs: food, shelter, love and relationships. Most of all, however, they need to learn how to manage their way in this world. They need to learn about how things work and how to have their needs met.

Often, some of their behaviours cause us (the parents) a problem:

- When they want to see what money feels like in their mouth, and then they swallow a coin.

- When they want to see what happens when you pull the corner of the tablecloth.
- When they want to see what happens when you pull your sister's hair.
- When they want to see where mum's mobile goes when you put it down the toilet.
- When they want to discover how loudly they can scream.

'Do not assume that your children are trying to do something to you, they are simply trying to do something for themselves.' —Dr Gordon

Often when I speak to parents at my seminars they express surprise at the fact that children are not manipulative and are not behaving in particular ways to annoy you or deliberately be naughty. There are a small number of older children who might misbehave deliberately but these are children who have been emotionally damaged and are not having their needs met.

There are some deep-seated beliefs about children, which might cause us to adopt an Authoritarian approach to parenting. Some of these beliefs include:

- *Children are attention seekers* and are deliberatively disruptive to gain attention. There is widespread belief that this attention seeking behaviour should be ignored and the child given less attention. A compassionate response to a child's need for attention and love would be to provide it.
- *If you give an inch they will take a mile.* This belief distrusts children's basic motives. There is no evidence to suggest that children are inherently wired to be selfish. A child's selfishness is a developmental process. Children learn to understand themselves before learning to connect and consider others.

- *Children are manipulative* and are out to get you. Again, there is no evidence to suggest this is true.
- *Spare the rod and spoil the child* is a well know proverb meaning if you don't punish your child they will be spoiled. Unfortunately, there is no evidence that children who are not punished are spoilt.

Although most people will not support these views about children, many act as if they are true. A girlfriend once spoke to me about her baby crying. She was (reliably) advised that attending to her crying baby would not be considered spoiling her, provided the child was younger than 11 months. Presumably, once the child was older than 11 months, comforting her when she was crying was going to spoil her.

PARENTS ARE REAL PEOPLE

As Dr Gordon pointed out, often adults take on the role of a parent when they have children. Parents are still real people so it makes you wonder why they refer to themselves in the third person, as mummy or daddy. Some parents feel that good mothers need to have endless patience or must always want to play with their child. They tend not to tell their children about themselves. They don't share that they have had a bad day at work as they believe it is not necessary to tell their children this type of information. However, in reality parents are real people and have real feelings. They have good days and bad days and they are not perfect.

Authenticity is critical to building trust and good relationships, so share with your children things about yourself—respectful parents are real and authentic.

Unfortunately, there is a culture of *telling stories* to children. Children ask legitimate questions and adults entertain them with stories about mythical creatures. There is nothing wrong with stories, just keep them for story time. Don't undermine your credibility with your children by being the one whom they don't believe.

HAVING NEEDS MET

So what are needs?

There are a range of frameworks that help us understand human needs. Here we will explore Maslow's Hierarchy of Needs, which was developed in 1954 based on a study of healthy people. It is a renowned model for human needs. Maslow suggested people were motivated to have their needs met and when lower-level needs were met people then sought to have their higher-level needs met.

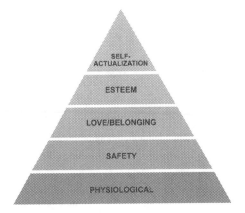

The cornerstone of an emotionally and psychologically healthy family is the concept of having everyone's needs met. We have the need for food, water and shelter. We all need love and to feel successful. At a higher level, we aspire to self-actualisation—the desire to contribute to society that for which we were put on the planet.

Humans are content when they have their needs met and are unhappy when they are not. If this is the case, they will seek to have their needs met so that they are happy.

Children have the same needs. They need food, shelter, love and the opportunity to learn about the world around them. In respectful families, both children and parents are having their needs met. Both parents and children work to help each other have their needs met and to live a fulfilled life while enjoying their relationships with each other.

Own your own problems

No-lose parenting

A respectful parent recognises that parenting is not a win-lose game; it is about recognising everyone has needs and we all deserve to have those needs met. This description of a No-Lose approach to parenting is drawn primarily from Dr Thomas Gordon's Parent Effectiveness Training. Dr Gordon was a counsellor and psychologist, and colleague of Professor Carl Rogers (the father of the humanist or client-centric approach to counselling and the father of modern counselling methods.) He was a pioneer in teaching communication and conflict resolution skills to parents, teachers and leaders.

Dr Gordon developed the concept of a behaviour window. He started with a rectangle. The marks inside the rectangle represented all of the behaviours our children exhibit.

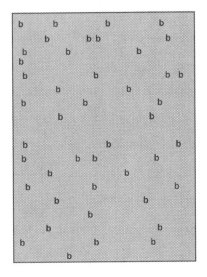

Accurate descriptions are important as they give the child a greater understanding of the behaviour you are describing. An example of this might be *you are leaving breakfast cereal all over the table.* This provides more data to the child compared with a judgement of *you're eating like a pig.* You know you have described the behaviour accurately if you can take a photograph or a voice recording of the behaviour. Compare the following:

'Why are you asking me a question when I am in the middle of talking to Dad?'

'You are rude'.

Of all of the behaviours in the behaviour window, some are acceptable to us and others are unacceptable. A behaviour is *acceptable* if it does not upset us. A behaviour is *unacceptable* if it annoys us and we want it to stop.

The behaviour window is then divided into two areas. A horizontal line across the rectangle is called the **line of acceptance**.

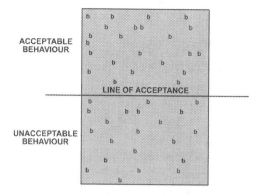

It's interesting that our **line of acceptance** can move up and down. Some days we are accepting of our children's behaviour and the following day we may be unaccepting of the same behaviour. We are not the same person from day to day. For example, my child persuaded me to buy him a drum kit and pay for lessons. When he practises, I am happy as I feel he gets something out of it and I have not wasted my money. His behaviour is acceptable to me. However, if I have a migraine tomorrow, then practising his drumming will no longer be acceptable to me.

This concept of a behaviour window and the fact that the line of acceptance can move leads to debunking a range of parenting myths.

FALSE PARENTING MYTHS

The respectful parent is not held hostage to a range of false parenting myths.

A united front is impossible

If each parent's behaviour window is different, then it is impossible to be entirely consistent. If I tried to adopt my partner's behaviour window, it would be inconsistent with how I truly felt.

It is impossible for parents to maintain a united front.

Most parents heave a sigh of relief when they truly understand that this is impossible. When parents try to be consistent regarding acceptable behaviours, they try to change their partner's mind about what they view as acceptable.

'Honey, you should not let the children jump on the couch.' If one partner disagrees with this rule, they will find it difficult to enforce this behaviour, as internally they don't really care if the child jumps on the couch or not. Trying to enforce this rule will lead to internal conflict and resentment towards the partner who persuaded you to agree to this rule. Parents will never be consistent and trying to maintain a united front will lead to conflict and result in confusion from the children.

I am often asked, 'Don't the children get confused with different rules?' My response is this: children deal with different rules all the time. There are different rules at school, kinder, Grandma's house, and their friends' house. Children just need to be informed about what is acceptable behaviour at each different location.

Being consistent is impossible

If we return to the behaviour window, we realise we are inconsistent from day-to-day. For example, on most days we are happy when our child is practising their drumming. After all, we have paid for the lessons, and we like to see our child making a commitment to the activity. However, if we have a migraine then this behaviour, all of a sudden, becomes unacceptable. Our behaviour window has changed. Maybe we think, even though I have a migraine I can't complain about the drumming practise as my child will get confused if I suddenly change what is acceptable. Therefore, I put up with it for a while but the behaviour is still unacceptable to me as it is causing me pain and I want it to stop. Eventually I will *blow my top* as the drumming practise causes me so much pain. Does my child wish to cause me this amount of discomfort? Of course not. They would rather know that the drumming was causing a problem and stop it for a while.

How we are feeling will change our behaviour window.

Our feelings on the acceptability of our children's behaviour will also vary depending upon the child. For example, we might think that it is acceptable for our 3-year-old to eat with their fingers but not our 7-year-old. Or we might think it is OK for boys to play in mud but not our girls.

Our feelings of acceptability will depend on the personalities or health conditions of our children. We might be more accepting of children with similar personalities to ourselves and less accepting of those who are different. We have a unique behaviour window for each child.

The environment in which we are operating also changes our behaviour window. For example, we might not mind if our children eat with their fingers at home—that behaviour is acceptable. However, eating with fingers is not acceptable when dining out with friends. Personally, I don't mind playing wrestling with my child at home but wrestling with him in public would cause me embarrassment. The behaviour goes from being acceptable to being unacceptable.

RESPECT IS EARNED, NOT GRANTED

Many parents ask about respect. 'My children should respect me because I am their parent. I respected my dad because he was my dad.'

The respect being described is what you would give a poisonous spider. There is nothing you like about the spider but you respect its ability to cause you harm; therefore, you keep out of its way.

As parents, we love our children, and we want the best for them. However, in adopting the parenting style of *our* parents, and using punishment and rewards, we lose the respect that our children gave us when they were tiny— when we were so capable and powerful compared to them. Every time we punish our children we chip away at this respect, we fail to replace it with respect that comes with listening to a child, acknowledging their needs, guiding them towards appropriate behaviour and modelling the behaviours, and values that we would like them to emulate.

Through parenting with punishment and rewards we not only damage our relationship with our children, we lose our influence. When we lose our influence, we lose total control.

Respect is earned and not bestowed.

Whose problem is this anyway?

One of the key skills to respectful parenting is understanding who owns the problem within any interaction.

When our child is upset, or not having their needs met, they have a problem. If a parent finds their child's behaviour unacceptable (to them), the parent has a problem. Each of these combinations are represented below.

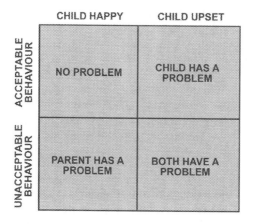

No-problem area

The top left box is the *no problem* area. The parent finds the child's behaviour to be acceptable and the child is also happy. For example, the parent is reading a book and the child is patting the dog, or the family is happily watching TV together or playing cards.

The child has a problem

In the top right box, the child is upset; they are *experiencing a problem*. The child is not having their needs met. For example, the child may come home from school crying because they have no friends, or the child might be frustrated because they cannot piece their Lego together.

The parent has a problem

In the bottom left box, the *parent* is finding the child's behaviour unacceptable and is experiencing a problem but the *child* is happy. For example, the parent might have discovered that there are biscuit crumbs all over the lounge room floor but the child is happy in the study playing with their Barbie dolls.

Both have a problem

Finally, in the bottom right box both the parent and child are experiencing a problem. The parent finds a behaviour which is unacceptable and the child is also unhappy. For example, you want to go camping for the weekend and your child wants to go to their friend's birthday party.

Respectful parents recognise who owns the problem and do not make the mistake of taking on the child's problems or making their problem that of their child. The concept of problem ownership is critical, and the first skill that parents must learn is to identify who owns the problem in the relationship when any issues arise.

THE PROBLEM WITH SOLVING OUR CHILDREN'S PROBLEMS

You must first recognise your child is experiencing a problem. The problem belongs to the child. This does not mean we don't care that the child has a problem nor do we not want to help our child *own* it. It is not our job to solve the problem. Most of the parents who attend my seminars think that if their children are experiencing a problem then they, as the parents, must solve it.. This belief is particularly prevalent amongst mothers. When your child is a newborn baby, most of your child's problems are yours: your child is hungry; it is your job to feed it etc. However, this simply cannot translate to adulthood. A parent cannot solve all of their adult children's problems. Would you like your parents to be there to solve all of your problems?

When we try to solve our children's problems, we effectively do two things. Firstly, we deny them the practise and opportunity to learn to solve their own problems, and secondly, we send them a subtle message that they are not capable of doing so.

As parents, we tend to do a bad job of solving our children's problems. Our solutions are based on our (not their) experiences and we are not informed fully of all the information relevant to solving their problems. For example, we cannot truly know what is important to our children, and we do not have a sufficient amount of information to be able to come up with a good solution.

Also, we are not always with our children to solve problems that eventuate in school, at a friend's house, at Grandma's house. We can (and should never) be with our children all of the time to solve these problems.

Parents report that when they realise they cannot and should not solve all of their children's problems, they feel relief that the burden has been lifted. One mother expressed it like this, 'My children were fighting over breakfast this morning. I realised it was not my problem. I sat down and poured myself another cup of tea.'

Just to reiterate: it is not that we don't care that our child has a problem or is upset, we simply don't have to solve it. We will learn some powerful skills, which will enable us to facilitate our child to solve their own problems.

THE PROBLEM WITH PASSING OUR PROBLEMS ON TO OUR CHILDREN

Another key mistake parents make is to push their problems onto their child, which places an unfair burden on them. Let's say it is really important to you that you have a tidy house when your mother comes to visit. You are afraid if you have a messy house, your mother will judge you to be a *bad housekeeper* and a *bad mother*. You yell at the children because there are toys all over the floor—this is unfair on them. There are other ways to solve this problem including:

1. stop caring what your mother thinks
2. let the children create mess elsewhere
3. find other ways the children can have fun, which will leave you with a tidy house.

WE INVITED OUR CHILDREN TO STAY

The respectful parent recognises they invited their children to come and live with them and it is important to accommodate them. Have you ever noticed how some people treat guests with more respect than they treat their children? It is unfair and unreasonable to think you can invite a vulnerable child to come and live with you and not change your lifestyle and your home environment to accommodate them. A respectful parent works to have everyone's needs met. Sometimes this involves accepting that having an immaculate house is simply not compatible with the needs of young children.

WILLINGNESS TO LEARN

A respectful parent recognises they don't know everything. In fact, parents receive virtually no training for what is the most important job in their life. Respectful parents are open and willing to learn new skills to enable them to be better parents and open to new experiences and learnings from their children.

THE IMPORTANCE OF EMOTIONS

A respectful parent recognises that emotions matter. They are real, not to be feared, and we should not feel ashamed of our emotions. The respectful parent allows and respects the child's right to express their emotions.

The respectful parent is skilled at helping their child understand and safely express their emotions. The respectful parent understands, respects, and owns their own emotions. They are able to express their emotions with control, honesty and authenticity. The respectful parent recognises when they are not in control of their own emotions and when they need to do some work to manage them

Understanding of self

A respectful parent recognises that *who they are,* is as much, or more important, than what they say or do. Children will essentially model themselves on their parents (with influences from school and other important adults). This is the good news and the bad news. If you don't want your child to inherit your anxiety, don't try to hide it. Learn to manage and minimise it. If you don't want your child to grow up with a chocolate habit, then kick your own habit.

Observe *who you are* and if you don't like what you see, begin a personal development and training program.

Understanding children's capabilities

Growing up is a process of physical, emotional and social development, and it is unrealistic to expect children to do things they are physically, emotionally or socially unable to do.

For example, learning to control their bowels and use the toilet requires physical development. A child needs to understand first the *feeling* of a full bowel in order to then *recognise* that feeling and connect it with knowing it is time to use the toilet. Punishing children for pooing in their pants is simply cruel.

It is unreasonable to expect a 2-year-old to share their toys. It is unreasonable to expect a 3-year-old to remember how to cross a road safely.

It is unreasonable to expect a prep-aged child to be able to read competently.

Children are not misbehaving when they are developmentally unable to complete a task or understand a concept.

EXPECT MISTAKES

Childhood is about learning new skills. Learning, by definition, requires us to make mistakes. If mistakes aren't made, the child is not learning—they are practising a skill they already own. Your child has many things to learn about how their body operates physically: What happens when I try to stand up? What happens when I put my hand under a stream of water? What happens when I make a squealing sound? What happens when I push my friend over? For every activity they learn, they will make mistakes. Often these mistakes have outcomes that are *unacceptable* to us. They cause *us* a problem. Punishing children for their mistakes is unfair, and it *will not* prevent the mistake happening again. Mistakes will happen until the child learns the skills they need to learn.

CHANGING HABITS

Have you ever tried to change a bad habit? Hard, isn't it? It is the same for children. My son is physical and loves to run and jump on me. It was funny when he was two; a little annoying when he was three; at four, it became a problem and had to stop. I communicated with him why it was a problem for me. He understood but he didn't stop. Now he jumps on me and says, 'Sorry mum, I didn't mean to'.

It is hard for a small child, overcome with the exuberance of the moment, to change their behaviour. Eventually they remember and they stop the unacceptable behaviour. Would punishing a child for making a mistake change the behaviour? No, but it would crush their spirit and damage your relationship.

LACK OF CLEAR COMMUNICATION

How often to you hear parents say, 'Stop doing *that*; if you do that again there will be trouble'. Have you ever wondered what *that* is? What behaviour does the parent find so objectionable? Have you ever heard the parent explain why the behaviour is unacceptable? As parents, we tend to provide very little information, to the child, on why their behaviour is objectionable. Maybe if the parent said, 'I get worried when you play tag around the BBQ. You may trip and burn yourself', the child would understand the situation and be in a stronger position to change their behaviour.

Many of our children's *misbehaviours* are a result of miscommunications between parent and child. Children have neither the understanding nor the vocabulary levels of parents. They need things to be explained clearly, so they can understand how and why their behaviour is causing a problem.

Why do we think everything has to be done our way anyway?

THERE ARE DIFFERENT WAYS OF DOING THINGS

A respectful parent recognises that often our children are not misbehaving: they are just doing things their way. When we ask them to clean their teeth, why do we get annoyed when they do not immediately stand up, go to the bathroom and clean them? Why should everything be done within our timeframe?

Why should the towels be hung straight away?

Why should the underwear be folded instead of being put straight into the drawer?

Why should decorative pillows be put on the end of the bed in a bedroom where no one sleeps?

Why does the dishwasher have to be emptied *now* rather than in half an hour?

Why do I have to have a bath every night?

As adults, we maintain beliefs and habits about how things should be done—usually in a particular way. This is important for the perfectionists in the house - those who need to make sure that the washing is hung with matching pegs and that the tomato sauce should be put back in the pantry in line with the BBQ sauce and with the label facing outwards.

It seems totally unreasonable for our children to be subjected to these standards when most of the time they make no logical sense. To the perfectionists in my classes, I ask: how would you like to live with someone who insisted that the washing be hung with multi-coloured pegs, when you think they should match? When children do not meet our *exact* expectations and within our *exact* timelines, they are not misbehaving. It is appropriate for our children to resist being controlled in this way and it would be wrong to punish them for not following our exact ways.

We invited our children to share our home. We need to move over and make room for them. We need not make them feel like they are intruders with no rights.

A No-lose attitude

A goal of the respectful parent is to spend a lot of time in the *no problem* area by reducing the amount of time spent in the other boxes.

It is not the number of conflicts that happen in a family, it is how those conflicts are managed that dictates the success, or otherwise, of a family.

Solving problems are a normal part of life. The goal is not to reduce the number of problems but to solve them, grow and move on to the next challenge. A respectful parent recognises that problems happen, and when conflicts arise they solve them and move on.

THE PARENTING TOOLKIT

The respectful parent has access to a full range of tools to enable them to parent for any eventuality.

The following toolkit offers all the tools you need to manage your relationship with your child without needing to resort to rewards and punishment.

	CHILD HAPPY	CHILD UPSET
ACCEPTABLE BEHAVIOUR	**NO PROBLEM** • Positive • Preventative • Declarative I-messages	**CHILD HAS A PROBLEM** • Passive listening • Active listening • Facilitated problem solving
UNACCEPTABLE BEHAVIOUR	**PARENT HAS A PROBLEM** • Confrontative I-message • Shifting gears • Changing environment	**BOTH HAVE A PROBLEM** • Problem solving • Modelling • Consulting • Changing self

The key to applying these skills is to:

- Determine who owns the problem.
- Select and use the right tool.

Chapter Five

SELF-MANGEMENT FOR THE RESPECTFUL PARENT

The respectful parent will learn key skills to enable them to manage themselves and communicate with their children in a respectful way. They are skilled at helping their children deal with their problems and their upsets, while clearly and authentically expressing their own emotions and needs. They respect the entire family's needs and work together with other family members to solve problems so everyone's needs are met. They share their values with their children in a respectful manner.

We are *only human*, and we get frustrated. We yell at our kids and sound just like our parents, against which we swore we would never be. We used to be calm and sane. We were in control and held down responsible jobs. What happened?

For some reason, having children has bought out the worst in us. They say that children don't come with an instruction manual; however, it seems they come equipped with a manual that details all our buttons so they know which ones to press ....

Self-management is a critical element to parenting.

UNDERSTANDING YOUR OWN NEEDS

Everyone must have their needs met in order to be satisfied.

We have already explored Maslow's Hierarchy of Needs. Here are Tony Robbins' six **basic human needs**:

1. Certainty: we need a basic level of certainty to avoid pain and gain pleasure. We need a roof over our head, clean air and water and sufficient food.
2. Uncertainty: if life is completely certain then we get bored. We need some variety.
3. Significance: we require a feeling that we are unique and significant in some way.
4. Connection: we want to feel part of a community, and cared for and loved.
5. Growth: we want to grow, develop, learn and improve our position in life.
6. Contribution: on some level we want to contribute back to life something of value.

Many parents, particularly mothers, realise they are not having their needs met. The key clue here is she is resentful towards her children and husband. Pushing aside your own needs for the sake of the children does not work. It leads to unhappy parents who are unable to be available fully to their children and who become angry and resentful towards their children (despite their best efforts).

Typical needs not being met include:

- time to oneself
- time with partner without the children around
- exercise
- social needs – being with friends
- financial needs – either for the family or for self
- independence
- feelings of achievement that might have come from work.

I remember talking to one mother—an artist. She had not painted a picture since her two children had arrived. Every day she yearned to paint a picture and every day she resented her children because she could not paint. She felt guilty because she wanted to paint. For this mother, painting would make her a happier and better parent.

MANAGING OUR OWN REACTIONS

A number of parents, who come through my program, observe in themselves a tendency to react before thinking and be *so* upset by their children's behaviour that they are unable to be present for the child and to actively listen to them. They have the skills to do so, but find they are not in the right emotional state to be able to help have their children's needs met. When the children's needs are not being met, the parents will find that the children will not be in a place to help the parents have their needs met either.

Our brains have a basic design flaw; this is a result of our evolutionary history. There are three layers in our brain. Our *reptilian* brain governs our instincts. My son calls it our *lizard* brain. Then we develop our *emotional* brain, which gives us the capacity to love and care for our young. Next, we develop the *neo-cortex*, which makes us human and gives us the unique ability to think rationally.

When we become upset or scared our lizard brain fires up first and we act on our instinct and do *dumb things* that we regret later; we are not thinking rationally so we cannot apply a rational response to the situation.

There are a range of ways to handle this problem and to train ourselves to think before we react. It is not the intent of this book to describe all of these options but to raise the issue as a serious one, which is affecting the ability of parents to be there for their children.

THINGS YOU CAN DO IN THE MOMENT

Yogis talk about the space between an event happening and our response to it. Events don't make us respond. We choose our own responses. The problem, for most of us, is there is such little space between the event and our response that it feels like the event *made us yell*. So what can we do between the event and the response? Here is a list of actions we can implement *in the moment*.

- Take a deep breath.
- Relax your shoulders.
- Walk away until you calm down.
- Count to three in your head before you respond.
- Tap on the inside of your *pinky* finger to calm yourself.
- Imagine you are sending a pink puff of love from your heart to that of your child's.

THINGS YOU CAN DO TO LOWER YOUR REACTIVITY

There are actions you can implement when *not in the moment* that will improve your ability to remain calm, so you can respond appropriately.

It can be helpful to understand why we react so strongly to some of our children's behaviour. One parent identified conflict in her household when growing up, as the reason she became upset when her children fought at home. Simple awareness of these things can help.

Some of the options you may wish to include in your life:

- Meditation and mindfulness enable us to calm ourselves and be present for our children. (Napthali, 2010)
- Acceptance Commitment Therapy, which helps us accept our feelings then take action to improve our circumstances based on what is important in our lives. (Harris, 2008)
- HeartMath is a scientifically based methodology to reduce stress. (Childre, Martin, & Beech, 2000)
- Neuro Linguistic Programming (NLP) includes a range of techniques that take the *emotional sting* out of previous life events leaving us less reactive. Tony Robbins is probably the most well-known NLP practitioner.

Chapter Six

HOW A RESPECTFUL PARENT WILL LISTEN SO THEIR CHILDREN WILL TALK

$\mathbf{W}$e are now addressing how to help a child when they are experiencing a problem. Our goal here is to be a successful *helping agent* to help our child resolve their upset and have their needs met.

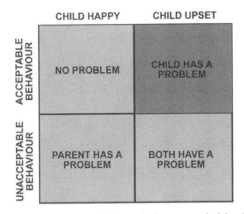

There are four key skills to help your child when they have a problem. They are:

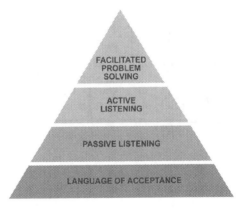

1. The language of acceptance (avoiding the language of unacceptance).
2. Passive listening.
3. Active listening.
4. Facilitated problem solving.

The attributes of the *helpful* parent

There has been significant research into how to help people when they are upset. What is clear from this research is it is not necessarily the techniques that helpers use, but their attributes that are important. It is estimated that 70 per cent of the ability of the helper (to help) comes from their attributes, which ensures there is a strong foundation from which the helper can help.

There are three essential attributes to being able to help your child. They are empathy, acceptance and authenticity.

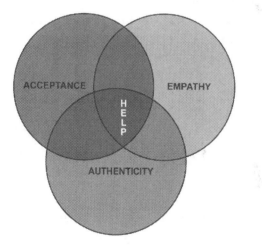

Acceptance

Acceptance of the person being helped is the key element in being able to help them. When a child feels accepted by their parents, they will open up. On the other hand, if a child feels unaccepted, they will shut down and not share with their parents. After all, would you share something with your parents if they were only going to judge, criticise, preach and moralise to you?

Acceptance means that we are OK with who our children are.

Acceptance means that we don't want to change our children.

Acceptance means that our children are already OK.

Sometimes we are not accepting of our children; that is OK. After all, we are only human. However, it does mean that we are unable to help our children at that time.

Accepting our children for who they are is not the same as accepting or approving of their behaviour. When we accept them, we can understand their behaviour better. This opens up the opportunities for change.

'It is one of those simple but true paradoxes in life: When a person feels truly accepted by another, as he is, then he is free to think about how he wants to change, how he wants to grow and how he can be different, how he might become more of what is capable of being.' —Dr Gordon

It is also true that you cannot *force* another person to change. You can only *influence* them. A person will be unlikely to change based on your *disapproval* as this will lead them to *dig in* and defend who they are. Your acceptance enables them to let go of who they are and move *on*.

If you want to help your child, then accept them for who they are (without wanting them to be different). If you are unaccepting then you are unable to help them with their problem at the time. Walk away and leave the helping to someone else or for another time (when you are accepting). It is impossible to be accepting of someone with whom you are angry. Walk away until your anger has dissipated, then you can help your child.

Empathy

Empathy is an essential element in helping your child with their problems or comforting them when they are upset.

It is about identifying with the person, putting yourself in their shoes and seeing the world through their eyes.

When someone feels your empathy, they sense your understanding of them. They feel listened to. To know you feel the empathy of another is a deep relief. It feels good.

Empathy is not sympathy. Sympathy is feeling sorry for the other person; it is about pity. While sympathy **separates** you from the other person, empathy brings you closer. Empathy leaves you feeling connected.

When we are feeling empathetic, we can listen deeply to the other person and this makes us feel more empathetic. It's like a perfect virtuous circle. It's like a feedback loop in a microphone that simply amplifies the empathy.

When I listen to my child, I am suddenly transformed into his world. This is the world of being a child, where things are sometimes hard; where often he struggles to understand how to spell a word or why a friend is mean to him. This changes my own attitude. It makes me want to help him feel better. This strengthens the bond between us.

Authenticity

The third leg to the attributes of a parent wanting to help their child is authenticity and it is critical to enable us to help and connect with a child or other person. You cannot help someone if you are not being *real, genuine, honest or authentic*. Being authentic is tuning the radio to the exact station, without distortion or static.

It seems obvious we should be authentic, doesn't it? Yet it is amazing how often parents are not authentic or honest with their children or don't tell them what is going on. Parents tend to take on the role of a parent. Instead of retaining our own identity, there is a tendency to see ourselves as a mum or a dad where we have preconceived ideas of what a mum or a dad should do. For example, mums must make sure their children go to bed at the same time each night, even though you might feel like letting them stay up tonight as there are friends over. Mums should not laugh at *bum* jokes, even though they might be funny. Mums should not let our children eat lollies, even though inside we might believe that it doesn't hurt once in a while.

Being honest and authentic has multiple benefits. It is impossible to build a relationship with someone whom we don't know. Relationships are strengthened when we understand the other person and we know that they are real.

Even more importantly, if we are not being genuine then we are untrustworthy. No one is going to open up to someone whom they don't trust. You cannot help someone if they don't trust you or if you are not being honest, genuine or authentic.

THE LANGUAGE OF ACCEPTANCE

Unfortunately, much of the language we use to help people when they are upset does more harm than good. Why? Firstly, I believe most people are scared of other people's strong emotions, such as fear, sadness and anger. Maybe we are afraid we will be affected by those emotions ourselves and they will make us feel bad. Maybe we just don't know how to deal with strong emotions because no one has taken the time to teach us.

Here are examples of things we might say when our child is upset or has a problem:

- Don't say things like that.
- Stop crying now.
- You will be sorry, if you do that.
- What you should do is....
- Why don't you play something else?
- We all must learn to get along with each other.

- It was your fault that happened.
- Well I think you did a great job.
- You are behaving like a baby.
- Big boys don't behave that way.
- You will feel different tomorrow.
- Don't worry, it will be fine.
- Why did you do that?
- Just forget about it.

Do any of those sound familiar? Often we have the best intentions and we want to help our children when they are upset but put yourself on the receiving end of some of these statements and ask yourself if they would be favourable to you?

Most of the language we use to help people when they are upset, blocks communication from the upset person and prevents them from processing their feelings and working out how to solve their problems. Most of the language we use has a subtle and underlying message. Consider these:

- There is something wrong with you because you have this problem.
- You are not smart enough to work out how to solve this problem so I have to tell you how.
- I don't want to hear your emotions because they make me feel bad.

If these examples demonstrate unacceptance of our children, we need an alternative language to demonstrate our acceptance of them.

SILENCE IS GOLDEN

I happen to believe that we live in a world where no one really listens to anyone else. I think that is why we have so many counsellors and psychologists; you have to pay someone to listen to you.

To demonstrate active listening to your child is:
- *Stop* what you are doing and demonstrate, with your body language, that you are actually listening. Provide eye contact
- Turn towards your child.
- Offer to listen to them: 'Would you like to talk about that? I can listen, if you want'.
- Offer acknowledgments that you are listening: nod, give verbal cues like, 'Hmm' and 'I see'.

Remain silent. Most people listen long enough to work out what will be said next, and then wait for a gap in the conversation to enable it to be said. Parents are too quick to tell a child what to do. This is not listening. This is lecturing. If you are quiet, it gives the child the opportunity and space to say what it is they need to express.

Steve Covey, author of *The Seven Habits of Highly Effective People* says, 'When you really listen to another person from their point of view, and reflect back to them that understanding, it's like giving them emotional oxygen'.

ACTIVELY LISTENING TO YOUR CHILD

Mostly, I hear parents say, 'Of course I listen to my child'.

However, active listening is a much more powerful tool in demonstrating your acceptance of your child and helping them solve their problems. Active listening involves:

- passive listening
- listening for facts and feelings
- Feeding facts and feelings back to your child.
- demonstrating empathy and acceptance.

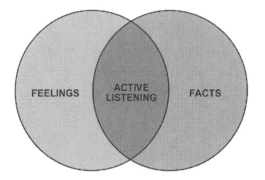

The most important element of active listening is listening for feelings and emotions. This is what separates active listening from other types of listening.

Let's look at some examples:

Child:	When is dinner?
Child's feelings:	Hunger
Active listening response:	It sounds like you are hungry.

Child:	Will the bike ride take long?
Feeling:	Worried about whether they are going to get tired.
Active listening response:	You are worried about getting tired on the bike ride.

Child:	Mary took my doll.
Feeling:	Angry because they want their doll back.
Active listening response:	You sound really angry and you want your doll back.

Child:	Crying
Feeling:	In pain from falling over.
Active listening response:	That is really hurting.

Child:	Crying
Feeling:	Sad because they can't have a lollipop.
Active listening response:	You are really sad because you can't have a lollipop.

Here is a typical conversation between a parent and child:

Child:	Mum, I didn't have anyone to play with today.
Parent:	What did you do?
Child:	Nothing.
Parent:	You should have found someone to play with. Where was Roger?
Child:	I don't know.
Parent:	You have to try harder to be nicer to people and make friends.
Child:	I am nice to people, they're just not nice to me. (storms off)

Here is a sample of a parent using active listening:

Child:	Mum, I didn't have anyone to play with today.
Parent:	That must have made you sad.
Child:	Yes it did. All the others were playing *gang-up tag* and I didn't like it.
Parent:	You sound really disappointed at that.
Child:	Yes. I was sad with no one to play with.
Parent:	So it sounds like you were a bit lonely.
Child:	Yes I was, maybe I can take a book to read tomorrow?
Parent:	You think that maybe if you took a book at least you would have something to do at lunchtime?
Child:	Yes but I would still like someone to play with. Maybe if I took my footy cards I could swap them with the grade 1 kids? (Thinks) Yeah, I think I will take footy cards and a book just in case.
Parent:	So it sounds like you have a plan for tomorrow.
Child:	Yeah.

Active listening gives you something to say and do when your child is experiencing a problem. It enables you to be helpful in a constructive manner. Usually after active listening, the parent and child feel closer. Active listening with your child helps you build your relationship through acceptance and listening—all you have to do is listen. Through knowing that your child's problem is not yours to solve, you can relieve yourself from the pressure and anxiety of trying to solve the problem. As the parent, you will know that active listening is the best approach to help your child solve their own problem. You can also relieve yourself from the pain of feeling your child's emotions, knowing that active listening will relieve them of these as well as empowering them to solve their own problems. Active listening is not only a beautiful gift to children; it is a beautiful gift to their parents.

Parents often ask me: What if I get it wrong? What if I say, *you sound really sad about that when really they are angry?* If you get it wrong your child will correct you and you will be appreciated for your empathy by listening to them. They will most likely say: 'No, I wasn't sad, I was angry'. This gives you the opportunity to say, 'It sounds like you were *really* angry'. Now they will feel you have listened.

By listening, your child will have processed their feelings and (more often than not) solved their own problem.

Active listening is a relatively easy skill to understand and once learned is easy to apply. However, it does take practice to learn a style of listening, which for many of us is entirely different from what we are used to.

Benefits of active listening

There are many immediate, short and long-term benefits of active listening to both the parents and the child.

	BENEFIT TO CHILD	BENEFIT TO PARENT
IMMEDIATE	Feel listened to Feel accepted	Feel closer to your child Child feels warmer to you
SHORT TERM	Emotional relief Problem solved	Problem is solved Relief from child's emotions
LONG TERM	Learn to understand own emotions Learn to understand others' emotions	Child will listen to you Better relationship with child More influence with child

THERE ARE SOME PITFALLS IN ACTIVE LISTENING

It is essential, when you are actively listening to your child, that you feel accepting of your child (in that moment). If you are upset or angry, active listening will at best be ineffective and at worst be considered manipulative by your child.

Some parents are tempted to use active listening to probe their child and discover the root of the problem. They continue with a *roadblock* such as preaching or moralising. This will reduce trust between you and your child and will most likely lead to them being wary the next time you listen to them.

Active listening helps the child process their own emotions and gain a greater understanding of their problem. Actively listening allows them to solve approximately 90 per cent of their own problems—we can facilitate them solving the remaining 10 per cent.

HELPING YOUR CHILDREN SOLVE THEIR OWN PROBLEMS

When your child has a problem and you have actively listened to them, they will have either solved the problem, or understood that they have a problem. Then you can facilitate your child to solve the problem:

Here is a 3-step problem solving technique:

1. Identify the problem.
2. Brainstorm the ides.
3. Choose a solution.

Step 1 is identified through active listening already acted out with your child.

Step 2 requires identifying options for solving the problem. The prime rule in brainstorming is *not* to evaluate ideas as you go along. Start by saying 'How do you think you could solve this problem?' and follow up with, 'What other ideas do you have?'

Parents find the most difficult part of this process is to avoid the temptations to provide their own ideas (especially as we are all think we are such good problem solvers). Younger children are often unable to think of any ideas. I advise parents to give the child time to come up with ideas. If, after some time, they are not able to come up with any ideas, ask your child if they would like some ideas from you; make sure you come up with a few ideas, from which they can choose.

Step 3 involves deciding what solution to implement. Ask your child, 'Which idea do you think like best?' Remember, the key principle in this process is that you are *facilitating* a process that enables your child to solve their own problem; it is *not* your job to solve their problem. Learning this skill is invaluable for your child, and they will learn this process on their own.

Sometimes your child will come up with an idea that is unacceptable to you—we will cover that next.

Chapter Seven

HOW A RESPECTFUL PARENT COMMUNICATES, SO CHILDREN WILL LISTEN

One of the things I love most about No-Lose parenting is that it acknowledges that both parents and children deserve to have their needs met. This chapter covers the *parent* having a problem and having the *parents'* needs met.

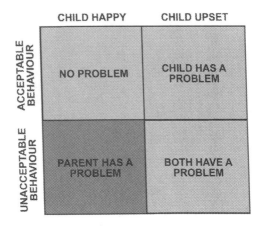

Changing the environment

The quickest (and lowest risk) strategy to having your own needs met is to change the environment in which you operate. For example, if you are on the phone and the kids are watching TV loudly, rather than yelling at them to turn it down you can simply take the phone into the other room. I know this sounds rather obvious but sometimes the obvious is not **so** obvious when our first instinct is to get the children to change.

I changed the environment in our house by purchasing two alarm clocks. When we only had one, I had control over it, which meant that every night I had to ask my husband what time he wanted it set. If I didn't set the alarm myself I would feel anxious as to whether it would be set. With two alarm clocks, I only had to set the alarm if I needed to. This is obvious to others, but it wasn't to me.

Examples for changing the environment include:

- childproofing unsafe areas
- providing appropriate storage space for toys and books
- getting a new chair that makes it easy for the child to eat comfortably
- designating places for your child to leave their toys so they don't have to be packed up all the time
- making sure your child can reach cups and plates, so they don't need to ask you.

I encourage you to address some of the recurrent problems in your house and think about how you can change the environment to solve your problem.

Changing self

Change yourself is the next strategy in having *your* needs met. Consider the following: How important is it, to me, for my child to do...? How important is it, to me, that they do it right now? How important is it, for them, to do it the way I want it done?

When you understand your own needs and when you observe yourself, you will often find that you can make problems go away by changing the way you think about things. For example, perhaps you want your child to have a bath now. Your child doesn't want to stop everything and have a bath now—they hate baths. If you take a step back and think about it, you might decide that one bath every two days is OK, perhaps they can have a shower instead. Does it have to be done right now? Perhaps before 8 pm would be OK? Perhaps you could wipe them down with a washcloth. All of these adjustments will reduce the conflict between you and your child and will leave your child feeling less controlled and less bossed around. It will give your child an opportunity to exercise their need for independence and autonomy.

A participant in my program believed that everyone should come to the dinner table wearing a shirt. She had grown up in a family where this was the rule. But with three boys and a pool this mother found herself having to enforce constantly the *must wear a shirt at the dinner table* rule. When she thought about changing herself, she realised that her *rule* had no real validity. When she let go of the *must wear a shirt at the dinner table* rule, she released herself of the burden of enforcing the rule and her children of the burden of following the rule. It is worth examining some of your beliefs to see if some can be changed without compromising your core values.

How not to get your children to change their behaviour

Many parents aim to have their own problems solved by getting the child to change their behaviour.

- Tidy up your toys.
- If you don't move your scooter, I will put it in the rubbish bin.
- You never help around the house.
- Turn that TV off.
- Do you think a maid lives here?

How would you (did you) feel and respond if your parent used this sort of language to you.

CHANGING PROBLEM BEHAVIOUR

Sometimes our children demonstrate behaviour that is unacceptable to us. The key tool used to change this behaviour is the Confronting I-message. *I-message* describes *my* experience (from the first-person point of view, and use of the pronoun I) as opposed to the statement that is based on *you*. *Confront* simply means *face to face*: to address the issue rather than ignore or avoid it.

A confronting I-message contains three parts:

1. an accurate description of the child's behaviour
2. a description of the impact the behaviour is having on you
3. a description of how this behaviour is making you feel.

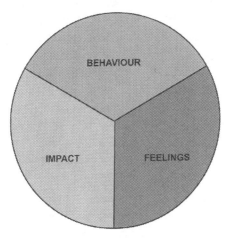

Let's explore each part of the I-Message.

Firstly, it is important that we describe the behaviour of a child. A behaviour is something you can see or hear. For example, your son pulling your daughter's hair is a description of behaviour. If you were to say that your son is *naughty,* you are putting a **value** description on the behaviour; you are not describing it.

If you are unsure whether you are describing behaviour, ask yourself, *could I take a photograph of this behaviour* or *could I record what is being said*? Why is it important that we describe the behaviour accurately? If a child is to change their behaviour, they need an accurate description of what they have done to cause a problem. If you just say, 'Stop being naughty' the child does not understand what part of their behaviour is considered naughty. Children need concrete data on their behaviour.

The second part of the I-message involves describing the effects of your child's behaviour on you. These effects are specific, for example, a waste of your time, a monetary cost, inconvenience; it has hurt you or damaged your belongings or causes you to not have your needs met.

The third part of the I-message involves describing how their behaviour makes you feel. Examples of feelings could include embarrassment, helplessness, sadness, worry, frustration, hurt, anger. It is best to avoid using the feeling of anger as the child feels it is pointed towards them. Try to identify the primary feeling that is causing the anger. Is it hurt, embarrassment or fear?

Let's look at an example of how to construct an I-message:

1. Behaviour: Leaving dirty washing all over the floor.
2. Impact: 'I' have to clean it up which wastes my time.
3. Feeling: Frustration.

So the I-message would sound like: 'When you leave your dirty washing on the floor, it looks messy and 'I' have to clean it up. This is frustrating for me'. This is significantly more palatable to a child than: 'You are a messy slob. Come and clean up this mess straight away'.

I-messages work in that you have provided the child a sufficient amount of information on why their behaviour is causing you a problem and its impact on you. Additionally, it is harder to dispute how someone is *feeling* compared with a 'You' statement, which can simply be disagreed with.

Note also that an I-message does not include an instruction to your child. You leave your child with the opportunity to decide upon an appropriate solution to your needs not being met. Most children actually do want to help you out, as long as their own needs are also being met.

Sometimes I-messages don't work

There are two key reasons that I-messages don't work.

1. The child is expressing a strong need.
2. There is a conflict in values.

The child has a strong need

An 'I' message may cause your child to have a problem. You say, 'When you leave your dirty washing over the floor, it looks messy and 'I' have to clean it up. This is frustrating for me'. Your child might respond with, 'I don't care, you are too fussy about mess anyway'.

A response like this is code for stop picking on me. This is an indication that now your child has a problem and they are upset. It means that we thought we had a problem when, in fact, both the parent and child have a problem.

In this instance, we need to **switch gears** and start to actively listen to our child in recognition that they have a problem. Then we can move onto problem solving laid out in the next chapter.

The child does not 'buy' that their behaviour causes you a problem

When we fail to identify that a behaviour is having a *real* impact on us, we are experiencing a conflict of values, which is evident when we use phrases like, *should, ought to* and *I don't know why. It is just the way it should be done.* It is often our beliefs about how things should be done that create conflict with our children: making beds, doing your reader as soon as you get home from school, eating all of your dinner. We will discuss how to deal with a conflict of values in the next chapter.

Chapter Eight

HOW RESPECTFUL PARENTS SOLVE PROBLEMS

WHEN YOU AND YOUR CHILD HAVE A PROBLEM

Sometimes we find that both parent and child have a problem or a conflict of needs. The child wants to go to their basketball game on Friday night and the parents want all the family to dinner at Auntie Ruth's house. It looks like we have a conflict and only one person can get their way.

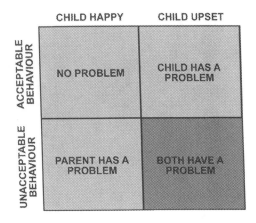

It is critical we discover the underlying needs of the parents and child, to identify an effective problem solving method that would meet the needs of both parties. There are four steps:

1. Understand needs of both parties.
2. Brainstorm alternative solutions.
3. Evaluate solutions.
4. Choose solutions.

In *step 1* the key is to separate needs from solutions. Needs might be to *socialise with friends*. A solution might be to *go to a party on Saturday night*. The needs of the child can be identified using active listening. The needs of the parent can be communicated using an I-message.

For example, with the baseball training conflict above, each party may have the following needs:

Parents:

- You want to spend time together as a family.
- You want to see your sister.
- You want to ensure your son sees his aunt.

Your child:

- They want to socialise.
- They don't want to let the team down.
- They want to play basketball.

In this step, you will spend most of your time problem solving. Another way of separating needs from solutions is to ask, 'What would that do for you?' and 'What would that do for me?'

For example, if your husband said, 'I want to buy a boat', his solution is to buy a boat. If you asked, 'What would that do for you?' he might say, 'I can go fishing, or we can go on a sailing adventure, or I can get away from the bustle of the city on the weekends'. These are his needs.

In *step 2* you would work together to brainstorm solutions that would meet both party's needs. The rules of brainstorming include no dumb ideas and that you do not evaluate ideas until you have finished your brainstorming. The reason for this is when you start evaluating ideas as they are generated you shut down the flow of discussion and discourage your child by dismissing their ideas. You can start by saying to your child, 'What suggestions do you have, which would make us both happy?' They say, 'What other ideas do you have?'

Some possible solutions may include:

- Go to Aunt Ruth's without your child.
- Change the date of dinner with Aunt Ruth.
- Change the time of dinner and we will pick you up from basketball, go straight to Ruth's and you can shower there.
- Get Ruth to come to our place for dinner, as it is closer to the basketball match and your son will be home on time.
- See if your son can play for the other team this week, which has an earlier match scheduled.
- Ask Aunt Ruth to watch the game and then take her out to dinner.
- Call the coach to see if they have enough players without your son.

In *step 3* you evaluate the options. Go through the list and identify which ideas would work for both of you. For example, it may not be acceptable to you to invite Aunt Ruth to dinner at your place, as you are tired and can't face having to prepare a meal for guests on a Friday night. You might say, 'That option won't work for me. I am too tired to cook dinner for guests on Friday night. What other options will work?' If you have written the options down then you can place a tick or a cross against each option. If you end up with no ticks, then go back to brainstorming or see if you can modify one of the options that meet *most* of the needs.

In *step 4* you choose the most appropriate option. The option of changing the time of dinner, then picking your son up from basketball and going straight to Ruth's could certainly work. It is important to remember that the solution to each problem is going to be unique to each family.

This method of problem solving can be used to solve a range of family problems like the distribution of housework or where to go on holidays.

No-lose problem solving can also be used to address issues on the spot. For example, you might use a confronting I-message to communicate where you are not having your needs met and in doing so might trigger an upset from your child. You might actively listen to your child, and determine that both of you have a problem. You can say to your child, 'It sounds like we both have a problem. Can you think of a solution to this problem, which will work for both of us?' I find the majority of problem solving in our house, is of this nature.

Children love problem solving. They love the fact that they get to express their needs and are amazingly creative when it comes to solutions. As parents, we tend to think that we already know the best solution to the problem, when your children will usually help you come up with a better one.

HANDLING CONFLICTS OF VALUES

Parents can have conflicts in both needs and in values.

Sometimes we find that when we try to put together our 3-part confronting I-message, we are unable to identify the real impact on us. Let's go back to our example of the *must wear a shirt at the dinner table* rule. The parent, in this example, realised that she was unable to determine the real impact on her if her children did not wear a shirt to the dinner table; she thought that was the way things should be done. This is an indicator that she did not have a conflict of needs with her children; she had a conflict in values.

So what are values? Values are beliefs we hold about how things should be or how things should be done. Our values define who we are and have been adopted by us through our life experiences. We adopt many of our values from our family of origin and modify them as we journey through life. Some of our values are held deeply, for example, stealing is wrong. Other values are held less deeply like the belief that everyone should wear a shirt at the dinner table.

When we have a **conflict of needs**, we use the problem solving method as described in the previous chapter. When we have a **conflict of values**, we need a different set of tools.

You cannot make another person adopt your values but you can influence your child's behaviours.

There are four key tools to influence values.

1. Share your values.
2. Consult.
3. Model.
4. Modify yourself.

Option 1 – share your values

Simply sharing our values with our children will help influence theirs. The tool we use here is a *declarative* I-message where we simply declare things about ourselves: what we think and what we believe.

- I think exercise is really important and I love to exercise by riding my bike.
- I think that when you meet someone you should look them in the eye.
- I don't like the cold; it makes me feel miserable.
- I love the month of July as I can watch the Tour de France.
- I hate seeing tattoos as I think it is like writing graffiti on your body and they are really hard to remove if you don't like them later on.

There are many opportunities to share your beliefs with your children.

Option 2 – consulting

This option involves a discussion with your child around the particular value that you are addressing. First, you must *be hired,* by your child; your child must be willing to listen to you. Ask if you can share something with them. If they say no, then you have to respect that and find another time. If you keep talking to them when they are not willing, you will come across as lecturing them—all they will hear is blah blah blah....

When you have been *hired* by your child (they agree to listen to you), you can explain your reasons for the values that you hold. For example, you might be talking about the importance of eating vegetables or academic achievement. You must be prepared with facts and figures so you may need to do some research prior to the discussion. You must clearly express your thoughts and back them up with real data. Finally, you must leave responsibility for change to your child. You get one go at this. Do not repeat and nag as you may not see instant change and you may never know the impact of your conversation.

Your child will be much more open to being *hired by you* as a consultant if you have a good relationship with them. If you listen to them they will be more likely to listen to you. If you lecture and preach to them, they will not listen and this tool will be ineffective.

Option 3 – model

Although we tend to focus on how our values differ from those of our children, when you look at it objectively most of our values are passed onto our children. In fact, children are wired to model what you do so they will *do what you do* and generally *ignore what you say*. If you want your children to be honest, *you* must also be honest. There are many cultures where parents do not actively teach their children as they know their children will simply model their behaviour and values.

If you maintain a quality relationship with your child, they are more likely to model themselves after you. Think about it: Do you ever take on the values and beliefs of someone whom you do not respect?

Option 4 – modify yourself

The final option is to modify yourself. Examine your value. Ask yourself:

- What is my value?
- Where did my value come from?
- Does my value *still* serve me well?

If the answer is yes, then you can use this information in your values discussion with your child. If the answer is no, you may be able to discard or adjust your value from a values collision to a values difference.

You can also *try on your child's values*. Try listening to their favourite TV shows. I was horrified when my young son first started watching Star Wars but now it is one of my favourites and we read Star Wars book together.

Modifying yourself may sound like a lame way of changing your children's values. But remember, you might be able to use power to make your child do something but you cannot use power to make your child think or believe something.

Chapter Nine

APPLYING THE SKILLS

In this chapter, we will look at how to apply these skills to some typical parenting challenges like tantrums, fighting, and getting your children to listen to you.

TANTRUMS

When a child is throwing a tantrum, the **child has a problem** and we need to use the appropriate skills for this area.

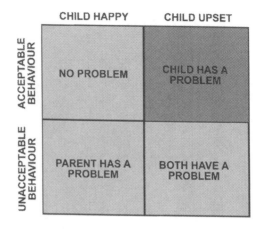

A tantrum is an extreme upset. It can take over their body completely, and they become *out of control*. It is akin to an alien taking over their body. The tantrum can be violent, intense and extremely distressing. For parents, they can be embarrassing and distressing, as we don't like to see our children that upset. We don't know what to do. When the tantrum happens in a public place, the distress heightens as others watch and we feel judged.

Neural pathways are like superhighways of nerve cells that transmit messages. When the child travels over the superhighway, many times, the pathway becomes increasingly solid. The child learns to react to things going wrong with upset and anger; therefore, the more tantrums they throw will increase the likelihood they will exhibit this reaction more in the future.

As children grow older, they might not have the *complete* tantrum but they will still be responding to things going wrong with a deep upset.

So what can we do? How should we help our children cope with their tantrums and learn better emotional control?

There is significant confusion over how we should deal with tantrums. Some try to reason with their child, while others use discipline. There is a school of thought, which recommends *not* rewarding a tantrum, as the child is seeking attention, and being manipulative and demanding. Others walk away from their child to let them calm down or simply because they don't know what to do.

I believe that when you walk away from a child throwing a tantrum, you increase their distress and fear. You add fear of abandonment to the already overwhelming emotions of the tantrum. When the child is in the holds of a tantrum, the rational part of the brain is not working. It has been overridden by emotions and the only response is emotional and instinctual.

I recommend you start by just being with your child. Sit with them while they cry. Hold them if they will let you. Remain calm. Your own anger and upset will increase the distress of your child. Dr Louise Porter recommends that with some children you should hold them firmly so they feel secure, especially if they are experiencing a violent tantrum. When they calm down enough for you to be heard, you can start actively listening to them. You can say, 'It sounds like you are really mad that you can't have that toy'. Or, 'You are really sad that Daddy has gone to work'.

Maybe your 3-year-old has had a meltdown because you gave them the blue cup and they wanted the pink cup. 'It sounds like you are really upset because I gave you the blue cup when you wanted the pink one.' For us it seems ridiculous; the blue cup works just as well as the pink one. Why do they have to get so upset? The answer is that, for them, is it important. It is also important for them to have some control over their own lives and environment.

Parents then ask me: 'Should I give them the pink cup?' Well, it depends. If you have a pink cup handy and it is no real problem, then why wouldn't you? If it is a real problem to give them the pink cup then obviously you can't. If it is a real impact on you because you have to go upstairs to get the pink cup and you don't want to, then don't. Some parents worry about being a doormat and that pandering to them is teaching them to be demanding. They tell me, 'Children have to learn that they cannot get their own way all of the time'. My answer to this is that there are plenty of opportunities for children to learn that they cannot get their own way all of the time.

Active listening can also be used to *prevent* tantrums. If you tune into your child's speech, body language and facial expressions, you can often detect that they are upset before it turns into a full blown tantrum. We can say, 'You really want me to stay home with you today'. Often that is enough to prevent the tantrum from happening. Just the feeling of being listened to and the opportunity for the child to understand and express their feelings is enough for them to calm down.

Remember that active listening will not completely solve a problem if *you* also have a problem. A child can have a meltdown because they are being prevented (by the parent) from doing something—from having a chocolate biscuit to wearing their favourite dress-up to kinder. In this instance, both the parent and the child have a problem and problem solving will be necessary to solve this problem.

CHILDREN FIGHTING

When children are fighting, we remain in the area where the **child(ren) has a problem**. The only difference is that it is two children – not one.

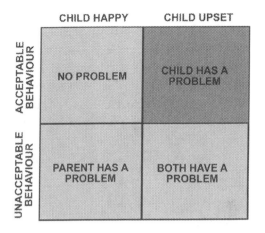

Unresolved arguments between siblings lead to growing feelings of resentment. These resentments build up over time if they are not resolved and can lead to deep feelings of anger between adult children. The behaviour of adult siblings, towards each other, can often be staggering in the depths of anger and the behaviour that it fuels.

Parents can easily facilitate conflicts between children and teach them to become competent at resolving their own conflicts.

Parents often find themselves becoming part of the conflict. It is like being infected by their disease rather than being quarantined from it. Parents listen to the conflict and decide who is the most deserving in the argument over a toy. They reward the *most deserving child* with the toy, and the *losing child* is left feeling angry and resentful towards you. It started as their argument and now your relationship with one of your children is negatively impacted.

The alternative is to actively listen to both children; yes, it can be chaotic. Then say, 'It sounds like you both have a problem. What ideas do <u>you</u> have to solve it?' The discussion will leave one or both of the children upset and you will have to actively listen to them to calm them down again. Then you can ask the same question again until you come to a resolution that meets both of their needs.

If you think that sounds like a momentous task, you are right. However, it will not take long for your children to realise that if they fight and you have to intervene, they will have to keep going through the same long and arduous process. Eventually, they will sort out their own problem.

The number one rule: don't join the argument. Let them sort it out or facilitate them to sort it out.

My children won't listen to me

Parents are deeply upset when their children don't listen to them. Some parents get their children's hearing checked only to discover their hearing is perfect. It's not that children are not listening; it's that they *choose* not to do what their parents are asking of them.

When the children are not listening to their parents, **the parent has a problem**.

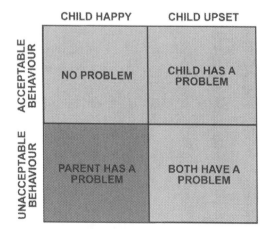

The first step here is to use a well-constructed I-Message. 'If you don't put your shoes on, we will be late for kinder and I will be late for work, which makes me worried my boss will growl at me.'

I think the above I-message will only have a 30 per cent chance of working.

Sometimes the I-message will work and sometimes it will not. There are two reasons for this.

- The child is trying to have a strong need met.
- The child does not buy the impact of the situation (on you). This is a values conflict.

If your I-message does not work then you **both have a problem**.

	CHILD HAPPY	CHILD UPSET
ACCEPTABLE BEHAVIOUR	NO PROBLEM	CHILD HAS A PROBLEM
UNACCEPTABLE BEHAVIOUR	PARENT HAS A PROBLEM	BOTH HAVE A PROBLEM

It is now necessary to *switch gears* and recognise that the child has a problem. Switching gears requires active listening, 'It sounds like you really don't want to put your shoes on and go to kinder'.

Keep actively listening until you have a good understanding of the **problem** and **need** of the child.

Now you can solve the problem, 'It sounds like we both have a problem. I need to get to work on time and you don't want to go to kinder. What do you think we can do about it?'

If your children are aged four and above and are used to problem solving, they might have some ideas. If they are younger, you will need to come up with several ideas from which they can choose. Be creative, open your mind and remain flexible.

However, I can almost hear you say, 'I don't have time for this. I have to get to work!' I certainly fell that way at times but I discovered that when I take the time to do this, it was actually a quicker solution. If I used my power and yelled or forced my son into the car, it usually took more time dealing with the tantrum and left me feeling upset and guilty because I had had an argument with my child.

Set aside a time when you are not under pressure to discuss recurrent problems with your child and see if you can come up with some ideas that might work for both of you:

- putting the shoes in the car then putting them on at kinder
- taking the favourite toy into the car
- making more time in the morning so the child does not feel under pressure.

APPENDIX

Evidence on the benefits of the No-lose Parenting Style

P.E.T. was first taught over 50 years ago. This has provided researchers sufficient time to gather evidence of the effectiveness of the program. This research can be accessed at www.gordontraining.com. A review of all of the research on P.E.T. by Robert Cedar of Boston University found:

- The overall positive effect of P.E.T. was significantly greater than the effect of alternative treatments.
- The greatest measurable effect was on parent attitudes.
- The effect of P.E.T. on parent behaviour was significantly greater than the effect of alternative groups.
- P.E.T.'s effect on children was greatest for the category of self-esteem.
- Parents did learn the P.E.T. concepts.

- P.E.T. parents improved their attitudes, showed greater understanding of children, increased their democratic ideals, showed increased positive regard, empathy, congruence, and respect for their children.
- P.E.T. children rated their parents as more accepting of their children.
- The positive effects of P.E.T. last longer than the eight weeks training. In fact, they lasted as long as a 26-week follow-up.
- P.E.T.'s positive effect on children increased over time.
- The magnitude of the positive effects of P.E.T. was greatest in those studies that had superior research methodology.

Diana Baumrind discovered that children who rated high in self-control and self-discipline were found to have parents who refrained from punitive punishment, using instead a reasoning approach; that is, messages that told the children the negative effects of their behaviour on others, as with the P.E.T. I-Messages. (Baumrind, 1967)

The most surprising evidence from this study had to do with changes in the IQs of the children as researched by Baldwin. Over the years, the IQs of the children with autocratic parents decreased slightly, while those of permissive parents remained almost the same. However, the IQs of the children of the democratic parents increased significantly over the years. The mean increase was over eight IQ points. The investigators concluded, 'It would appear that the democratic environment is the most conducive to mental development'. (Baldwin, Kalhoun, & Breese, 1945)

REFERENCES

Baldwin, A., Kalhoun, J., & Breese, F. (1945). Patterns of parent behavior. *Psychological Monographs.*

Baumrind, D. (1967). Child care practices antecending three patterns of preschool behavior. *Genetic Psychology Monographs*, 43-88.

Central, P. (2013). *Oppositional Defiant Disorder Symptoms.* Retrieved July 18, 2015, from Psych Central: http://psychcentral.com/disorders/oppositional-defiant-disorder-symptoms/

Childre, D. L., Martin, H., & Beech, D. (2000). *The HeartMath Soution: The institute of HeartMath's revolutionary program for engaging the power of the heart's intelligence.* HarperOne.

Chua, A. (2011). *Battle hym of the tiger mother.* Penguin Books.

Coleman, D. (2005). *Emotional Intelligence: Why it can matter more than IQ* (10th Anniversary ed.). Bantam Books.

Covey, S. R. (1989). *The 7 Habits of Highly Effective People.* US: Simon and Schuster.

Dictionary, O. (2006). Oxford University Press.

Doidge, N. (2007). *The brain that changes itself: Stories of personal triumph from the frontiers of brain science* (1 reprint ed.). Penguin Books.

Enten, R. S., & Golan, M. (n.d.). *Parenting styles and eating disorder pathology.* Retrieved from Science Direct: http://www.sciencedirect.com/science/article/pii/S0195666309000385

Harris, R. (2008). *The happiness trap; How to stop struggling and start a living: A guide to ACT.* Trumpeter.

Health, E. o. (n.d.). *Health of Children.* Retrieved July 18, 2015, from http://www.healthofchildren.com/P/Parent-Child-Relationships.html#ixzz3egtoZOoH

Helpline, K. (2015). Retrieved July 18, 2015, from Kids Helpline: http://www.kidshelp.com.au/grownups/news-research/hot-topics/family-relationships.php#sthash.8iryIzAE.dpuf

Napthali, S. (2010). *Buddism for mothers.* Allen and Unwin.

Porter, D. L. (2014). *A comprehensive guide to classroom management: Facilitating engagement and learning in schools.* Sydney: Allen and Unwin.

Porter, L. (2004, October 19). Retrieved July 18, 2015, from NSW Community News Network Archive: http://nswcnna.blogspot.com.au/2004/10/dr-louise-porter-on-protecting-children.html

Publications, H. H. (2001, December). *Harvard Health Publications.* Retrieved July 18, 2015, from http://www.health.harvard.edu/newsletter_article/the-health-benefits-of-strong-relationships

Robbins, T. (n.d.). Retrieved July 18, 2015, from Tony Robbins: https://training.tonyrobbins.com/the-6-human-needs-why-we-do-what-we-do/

ABOUT THE AUTHOR

Jenny is an author, trainer, coach, speaker and consultant who specialises in helping parents to enjoy parenting, and raise confident and resilient children. She interprets, for parents, what to say to their children.

After an executive career with Rio Tinto, KPMG and Yarra Valley Water, Jenny had a child at the age of 40. She founded Parent Central with the goal of providing parents a way of raising their children without using a system of threats, punishment and rewards. She helps parents with difficult or defiant children, parents who want to perform at their best, parents who want to enjoy great relationships with their children and parents who want to raise children with high emotional intelligence and excellent communication skills. Corporate Australia also benefits from working with Jenny by learning how to build great organisations by developing great managers.

Jenny is obsessed with the importance of how we raise our children. She believes strongly that children should be protected from the negative impact of parenting using a system of punishment and rewards. She is inspired by opportunities for parents to enjoy deeper and more intimate relationships with their children, and experience an enhanced opportunity to influence their children.

Jenny has a degree in Engineering and Environmental Science and an MBA from Melbourne Business School.

CONTACT

Jenny Bailey
jenny@parentcentral.com.au
www.parentcentral.com.au

Visit **www.parentcentral.com.au** to register for regular tips on how to be a respectful parent and avoid being fired by your children

Printed in the United States
By Bookmasters